The Novel and the Reader

GOLDENTREE BOOKS

KATHERINE LEVER
Wellesley College

The Novel
and the Reader

A PRIMER FOR CRITICS

New York
APPLETON-CENTURY-CROFTS, Inc

662-2

PRINTED IN THE UNITED STATES OF AMERICA

To Cora Medbury Lever
and John Howard Lever

Contents

Preface

Novels pour daily from the printing presses. Are they good or bad novels? Who is to say?

Advertisers try to persuade us that all new novels are good. Those we read, we soon discover vary from the very good to the incredibly dreadful. Our natural scepticism of the objectivity of a vested interest is so often confirmed by experience that our own powers of discrimination may be developed more in resistance to advertisers than under their guidance.

The advertisement does, of course, help a novel to sell. Are sales to be our criterion of value? The term *best-seller* has shifted in meaning from a statement of fact – "this novel is among the ten or fifteen novels selling most widely" – to a term of critical appraisal with the implication that the novel is good or bad depending on the tone of the speaker. For some a "best-seller" is a good novel which should be read as soon as possible; for others a "best-seller" is a vulgar novel to be avoided at all costs. Since the number of people buying a novel reveals popular taste, a reading of best-sellers may tell us much about our contemporary society. We must beware lest our repulsion for vulgarity become snobbishness. The popular taste is catholic: good novels as well as bad novels have become best-sellers. To refuse to read all popular novels because some are bad is as blind a prejudice as the desire to read any popular novel on the assumption that it must be good.

Reviews in newspapers and magazines help. Reviewers can warn us away from the patently bad and urge us towards the good. Nevertheless, the reading of a series of reviews about one novel quickly dispels any illusions we might have about their reliability. Reviewers often differ about the quality of a novel; even when they agree about quality, they may differ about the degree of the quality or about parts of the novel. Since the reviewers disagree, we can not trust any one of them to tell us in advance which novels are good, how good, and in what ways.

If we are to read novels at all, we need to be able to form our judgement of them independently. Our pleasure in reading a novel – and what other reason for reading a novel is more important than our pleasure? – is greatly enhanced if we are reading a good novel and know that it is good. We can give ourselves over to the novel with serenity, knowing that our pleasure is being derived from solid worth. When pleasure is based upon value, our taste is impeccable. If further we know that our taste is good, we have the security which is produced by self-confidence.

Pleasure, taste, value, and confidence are all products of knowledge. Knowledge of the art of the novel can be learned and can be taught. In some ways the art of the novel is simple, easy, and obvious. The novel is a modern and familiar form. Paradoxically, the very newness of the form and its very familiarity cause difficulties for the serious student of the art. These difficulties became clear to me the first time I taught a course in the art of the novel. Through the many questions students asked and by their comments on the novels we read, I gradually perceived that five basic questions called for answers if students were ever to discriminate with confidence between a good and a bad novel.

These five questions are:
1. What is a novel?
2. What is a novelist?
3. What is a reader of novels?
4. What is a critic of novels?
5. What is a student of novels?

These five questions are answered in the five chapters of this handbook, with the hope that students may lay a sturdy foundation for a lifelong love and understanding of good novels. The handbook is not intended for the dilettante whose taste is based on whim rather than value nor for the lazy who want to shut up thinking and discussion when they shut up a book. Nor is it intended for critics, professional or lay, who have already formed their critical standards. This is a handbook for students, for people of any age and occupation, who seriously want to learn how to tell a good novel from a bad. That such discrimination has both intrinsic and extrinsic value will, I hope, be clear to the student who achieves it.

The genesis of this book has followed a familiar pattern for academic books. Conceived in response to the needs of students, it has been fostered by the helpfulness of associates and friends, especially of Professor Ruth Michael. The librarians of Wellesley College, where most of my study has been done, and of the Baker Memorial Library of Dartmouth College, where I have worked for a short time every summer, have assisted me in finding the books I needed. The time for writing the book was provided by a new schedule of classes at Wellesley College, and the expense of typing the final copies was met by an award of the College.

The following publishers have kindly granted me permission to quote from copyrighted material: Cambridge University Press and Harper & Brothers for *Art and Reality* by Joyce Cary; Harcourt, Brace & Company for *The Second Common Reader* by Virginia Woolf; The Hudson Review, Inc. and The Ronald Press Company for "Technique as Discovery" by Mark Schorer, first printed in *The Hudson Review*, Vol. I, No.1, Spring 1948, Copyright 1948 by The Hudson Review Inc., and appearing in *Critiques and Essays on Modern Fiction*, edited by John W. Aldridge, copyright 1952 The Ronald Press Company; Charles Scribner's Sons for *The Art of the Novel* by Henry James as edited by Richard P. Blackmur, and for *The Story of a Novel* by Thomas Wolfe; and the Viking Press for *A Portrait of the Artist as a Young Man* by James Joyce, for *The Craft of Fiction* by Percy Lubbock, for *My Brother's Keeper* by Stanislaus Joyce, and for *Writers at Work, The Paris Review Interviews* edited by Malcolm Cowley. Paul R. Reynolds & Son, the agent for the James Estate, has kindly granted me permission to quote from "The Art of Fiction" by Henry James.

My parents have not only performed the normal parental duties of giving me their sympathetic interest and encouragement; they have also read the book with intelligence and common sense. It is in appreciation of their literary acumen and candid judgements that I dedicate this book to them as individuals whose opinions I respect.

Wellesley College
July 26, 1960

1 · What is a Novel?

Before we start consideration of the art of the novel, we should be sure we know what a novel is. I am not concerned with a verbal definition of a term, but with the analysis of our object. Analysis is essential for the student of literature because the nature of a book determines the way it should be read and criticized. Criticism can be neither intelligent nor fair unless the critic knows exactly what he is talking about. His first task is to be sure that the book in hand is in fact a novel at all. The nature of the novel being what it is, this task is more difficult than one might suppose.

The primary difficulty is that in common usage the word *novel* often denotes all types of book-length fiction. Used thus, the term applies to allegories like *Pilgrim's Progress*, satires like *Brave New World*, poems like *Troilus and Criseyde*, legends, fables, myths, folk-tales, and the many kinds of escapist fiction common today – detective stories, western stories, science fiction, and so on. Sometimes the term is extended to include a short story printed as a separate volume or a collection of short stories with or without common links. A one-word synonym for book-length fiction is convenient, but its use hampers the attempt to discriminate between good and bad novels. The various types of book-length fiction differ so much in purpose and effect that each type deserves separate consideration. One of the main aims of this chapter is to differentiate the novel from other types of book-length fiction.

Writers have not made our task of definition an easy one. Some of them are experimenters. They know what a novel is; they see its defining limits, and they view these limits as limitations. They try in their works to push the limits as far back as they can. One job of the critic is to determine whether the experiment has been a success. We must know the limits, so that we can.judge the quality of the novel in relation to those limits.

Did the writer aim at the novel? Did he aim and fail? Did he fail to aim? Did he aim beyond the novel? These are questions which can be answered only when we clearly understand what the novel is.

The history of the novel offers another explanation for the difficulty of defining the form. It has appeared late in the history of literature. Most of the literary forms of the western world were created by the Greeks. They had a very keen sense of artistic form and of due decorum in the individual artist's relation to the form. They were also followed by literary critics and historians who made rules and codified literature. The novel, however, developed in the eighteenth century when the word *original* was changing in meaning. Ian Watt states this concisely in *The Rise of the Novel*:

> We have seen that, from the mediaeval belief in the reality of universals, "realism" had come to denote a belief in the individual apprehension of reality through the sense: similarly the term "original" which in the Middle Ages had meant "having existed from the first" came to mean "underived, independent, first-hand"; and by the time that Edward Young in his epoch-making *Conjectures on Original Composition* (1759) hailed Richardson as "a genius as well moral as original", the word could be used as a term of praise meaning "novel or fresh in character or style".[1]

The novel has from its inception been free of traditions and conventions; it is *novel* or it is not a novel. Novelty must be part of the definition, and yet how can novelty by its very nature be defined?

Definition is difficult, but it is not impossible. The importance of definition should be a spur to our effort rather than a stumbling-block.

Definition is a two-fold operation. We define by saying both

[1] Berkeley and Los Angeles, 1957, p. 14.

what a thing is and what it is not. When we say a novel is a narrative, we are also saying that a novel is *not* whatever is not narrative. Usually we imply the negatives when we define, and we focus our attention only on the positives. In what follows, I am going to explain first what I think a novel is and then what I think a novel is not. The boundaries will thus be clearly marked on both sides of the dividing line.

A word of caution may be necessary here. No implication of value is intended by the definition. A book may properly be defined as a novel and be a bad book; another book may seem like a novel and by definition be proved to be another literary type and also be a good book. What can be said is that a novel to be a good novel must first of all be a novel. Because I am not depreciating the quality of a book by denying that it is a novel, I see no harm in strongly marked boundaries. *Troilus and Criseyde, Pilgrim's Progress, Gulliver's Travels* do not suffer from being regarded as a poem, an allegory, and a satire respectively; in my opinion they gain from being discussed in the terms proper to their kind and intention. They may be like novels in some respects, but they are not novels. We need to find out what novels are and then talk about their quality. This kind of intellectual discrimination has no connection with the rights of the individual in a democratic society; we are talking about literary types and not about human beings whose psyches can be damaged by lack of charity or justice.

My method of arriving at the definition I present has been a slow process of reading, thinking, discussion, and testing. I have read many articles and books on the nature of the novel. Particularly helpful has been what the novelists themselves have written about their art. I have correlated theories to find common denominators and then tested the common denominators by applying them to books generally considered to be novels. I have also tested the definition in conversation with relatives and friends and in the classroom with students. The definition I have reached now seems to me precise and as economical as possible, but I have no wish to assert its truth dogmatically. In the Appendix I have provided readers with a bibliography and suggested methods of testing the definition so that they may make their own decisions about any controversial points.

THE NOVEL DEFINED

A novel is the form of written prose narrative of considerable length involving the reader in an imagined real world which is new because it has been created by the author.

NARRATIVE

The novel is first of all, above all, below all, a narrative. That means that the novel is about action. For discourse about action the word *story* is popularly used. Like other common words, the word *story* has many meanings. Some people use it as a polite synonym for *lie*, and others use it loosely for *explanation*. The word *narrative* is more precise than *story* because it carries no connotations of untruth or factual statement.

Narratives, true or false, are loved by children and primitive people, by the uneducated and the unsophisticated. Some educated and sophisticated people regret this. Mr Forster, for instance, writes:

> Yes – oh dear yes – the novel tells a story. That is the fundamental aspect without which it could not exist. That is the highest factor common to all novels, and I wish that it was not so, that it could be something different – melody, or perception of the truth, not this low atavistic form.[1]

But is not melody "atavistic" too? Do not the simple of every age and time like song? Looked at from another angle, the curiosity of wishing to know what happened next is a universal human trait, one of the traits which distinguishes us from animals. The fundamental is necessarily *low* in one sense of the word but not necessarily *low* in value. Like Mr Forster I say, "the novel tells a story", but unlike him I omit the "oh dear yes".

People vary in their degree of curiosity. Some are interested

[1] *Aspects of the Novel*, London, 1949, p. 27.

in what happens only to immediate friends and family. Others are interested in what happens to any actual person. They read newspapers avidly and ask friends about friends of theirs whom they do not know personally. Still others can extend their interest to imagined people; among these readers will be found some who are interested in what happens in books but not to the man next door. What is important is the awareness that the reading of novels is related to a basic human interest in what happens to other people. This human interest may be a crude desire for excitement without danger, but it may also be an expression of sympathy, imagination, and unselfishness.

What happens in a novel is action. Action is basic but not simple. Action takes place in a physical world. The people acting have a physical appearance and they act in a physical universe. Thus narrative usually involves description, not as an end in itself but as a significant part of the action. For example, the action of a man running is not clear to us until we are told what the man looks like and where he is running. Action is often though not always accompanied with words. Moreover, words themselves may be a kind of action. The action of resigning, for instance, is the action of saying or writing, "I resign". Therefore, dialogue is added to description as part of narrative. The motives for the action are also important. Why did the man run? The explanation, "The man was frightened", is exposition. In a novel narrative is essential, and description, dialogue, and exposition are subordinate. In other forms of literature description, dialogue, and exposition may be essential and narrative subordinate. Some experimenters in the form of the novel try to see how little narrative they can write in proportion to the description, dialogue, or exposition.

Narrative is similar to drama in that both are basically concerned with action, but narrative differs significantly from drama in being *about* action rather than in being *represented* action. The drama is acted before our eyes by actors. We respond immediately to the actions of the characters because we see and hear them for ourselves. The tension arises from the interaction of actors and spectators heightened by the invisible wall between illusion and actuality which frustrates our desire to leap into the act to warn and help the actors. Narrative, in contrast, is conveyed to us by a narrator. We know only what the narrator chooses to tell us. His relation to what he is telling is a highly significant part of the tale. When we hear or read about an action, we are more or less consciously involved in who is telling us about it, why he is telling us, and how. We instinctively feel that he may not be telling us the whole story or the true story. The narrator's character and intelligence, his point of view and experience need to be taken into account. That a novel is a narrative, a discourse *about action*, is fundamental to our understanding of a novel and to the value we may derive from reading it.

WRITTEN

Narrative may be either spoken or written. In its spoken form it antedates history and continues today to be a staple of daily conversation among children as well as adults, the illiterate as well as the literate. Oral narrative is also a living art among ballad singers and reciters of epics. The novel may be distinguished from other forms of narrative because it is written to be read, not heard. Its rise in England coincided with the rise of a reading public and the rapid expansion of book publication. Novels have never been composed for recitation like other forms of narratives. This means that we do not hear the voice of the author. We recognize the tone of what he says, that is, the attitude he takes towards what he says, only through implication.

What we lose in tone, we gain in permanence. The voice of the author is brief. A new voice may alter the meaning of the words recited. The words on the page remain the same as long as the page exists. We know how children demand that the same words be used over and over again whenever a story is repeated. It gives one a sense of satisfaction, of rightness, of fulfilment which is stronger than curiosity. We know how difficult exact repetition is of a story told rather than written. Permanence can only be achieved through writing.

Writing means that the narrative is not dependent on the living presence of a narrator. It breaks the bounds of man's brief life and travels. The novelist can transcend time and space and communicate with thousands of readers all over the world and for centuries in the future.

A narrative committed to writing has a definite beginning and end. It shares with other forms of art in being a separate unit – a whole. The value of a novel is partly determined by the artistry with which the novelist begins and ends, his recognition of the limits within which he is working.

A written narrative means that the medium of the narrator is the symbol on paper, not the symbol of sound. He is using words as they will appear black on white, not as sounds to be spoken and heard.

If the narrative is written, it is not oral either in composition or in delivery. A novel is not an epic, even though epics like the *Iliad* and *Odyssey* have much in common with novels. A comparison of these epics with novels will quickly reveal the differences.

When we talk about the novel, we should always remember that the novel is a form of art and related to other forms of art in regard to aesthetic wholeness, that it is a form of literature and thus related to other forms of literature in regard to the medium of the word, and that it is written and thus designed to be communicated to the eyes of readers of many times and places.

PROSE

Novels differ from epics not only in being written but also in being written in prose rather than poetry. A narrative poem may be like a novel in every respect except this one and still not be a novel. An obvious difference between poetry and prose is that poetry is composed in lines as well as in words arranged in sentences. This is a difference in composition and not merely in typography. The lines may or may not have metre; the lines may or may not end with rhyming words; they may or may not vary in length. Nevertheless, the reader is aware of the rhythm of the lines as well as the rhythm of the sentences. Thus a poem has always at least one extra dimension that prose does not have. Poetry and prose differ in other respects, but these differences are less conspicuous and more elusive. One indisputable difference is sufficient for our purpose. While prose lacks the advantages of the extra dimension, it has a continuity poetry does not have. Prose seems less artificial and more realistic than poetry. Prose often gives the effect of being everyday speech. In this prose is deceptive. Prose is far from being everyday speech and is scarcely more realistic than poetry. Moreover, the writing of good prose is a great art. The very absence of confining limits, the very freedom of the English sentence, makes the writing of good prose as difficult as the writing of good poetry.

CONSIDERABLE LENGTH

The novel is long. The difficulty with including the term "length" in a definition is that it is a relative term. Unlike "narrative", "written", and "prose" – terms which are positive and reasonably precise – "long" has meaning only in relation to context. No arbitrary limit can be set at which the short written narrative becomes a long one, and I am not going to attempt to draw a line in terms of numbers of words. For the purpose of our study I am citing as examples only narratives of considerable length.

A natural question can be asked about narratives of medium length. Do they comprise a third genre midway between the short story and the novel – the novelette, for instance – or do a long short story and a short novel differ in genre according to some difference in content? Making distinctions of this sort helps some students to gain insight into literary form. For them I have provided a list of narratives of medium length by which they can sharpen their literary acumen. I personally think they comprise a third genre, but this opinion is an impression rather than a thoroughly considered judgement.

The important question to my mind concerns what the author does with the length given. Because the novel is long, it gives the novelist room to trace development over a long span of time, to encompass a wide scope, to delve deeply. Because the short story is short, it gives the short-story writer walls within which he can catch and hold the intensity of a moment, the fragility of an evanescent emotion, the shattering impact of a momentous discovery. Is the converse true? Is a narrative about a moment a short story no matter how many words are used or a narrative about a development over a span of time a novel no matter how few words are used? In my opinion the answer is no. Length regardless of the kind of narrative is part of the definition of a novel or short story. A novel is long. Experimenters in fiction may try to write novels about moments or short stories about development in time. The question then becomes one of quality. Is their novel a good novel? That is a critical question, not a question of definition.

AN IMAGINED REAL WORLD

The action narrated in a novel is imagined action. Narratives of fact are among the oldest of literary forms; we need remember only the histories of Herodotus and Thucydides to prove this point. Biographies, autobiographies, and confessions came later, but they all antedate novels by centuries. The narrator of facts tells what he believes has happened to actual people; the novelist tells what he believes happened to imagined people. Fiction is concerned with the real but not the actual.

Imagined characters may seem so real to readers that they become confused and think the novelist is writing about actual people. I know of one reader of Christopher Morley's *Kitty Foyle* who was so carried away by the vividness of Morley's imagination that he was confounded. He wrote a letter to a Philadelphia newspaper complaining about Morley's lack of veracity. I cannot quote his exact words, but in effect he wrote, "I have lived on Griscom Street all my life and never known a family named Foyle living here." The discerning reader knows that the characters in a novel do not have counterparts who exist in actuality. No records of birth, marriage, and death are available; no friends or relatives or descendants survive their death. Characters live only in the imagination of writer and reader.>

This may seem an obvious point, but it needs to be stressed none the less. Serious difficulties in the reading and criticizing of novels result from confusing novels with history, biography, autobiography, psychological case studies, sociological case histories, diaries, and journals. Most educated readers have been trained to check the veracity of a book by its correspondence with the actual. Such correspondence does not exist for the novel. The test for the reality of a novel is to be found within the reader. The novel as a form of art is self-sufficient.

Confusion is increased because novelists from the beginning have adopted the pretence of writing fact in order to make the imagined world seem real to the reader. Conversely, modern writers of non-fiction have adopted the techniques of the novelist to make their facts interesting and impressive. *Moll Flanders* seems like fact; *The Three Faces of Eve* seems like fiction. The discriminating reader is not deceived by appearances. He knows that Moll is a character and that Eve is a pseudonym for a person.

The relation of the imagined to the actual is a major psychological, philosophical, and practical problem. One aspect of the relationship is the relationship of the imagined characters to the actual people the author knew. A second aspect is the relation of these imagined characters to us as actual people. A third aspect is the relation between the people we imagine and the actual people we are in contact with. We are constantly striving to reconcile our images of people with the people themselves. The novel is significant because it is concerned with one of the most significant problems we face every day.

Some people accept readily the novel as imagined but deny it reality. To recognize that anything can be real which is not actual is a long step for them to take. Certain practical literalists insist that only the actual is real; anything imagined is unreal and untrue. They are the people who have added the connotation "lie" to the word "story". The distrust of fiction was strong at the time of the rise of the novel, and it is by no means absent today. Nor is this distrust confined to the ignorant.

The major difficulty in persuading anyone that an imagined world can be real is the myriad forms in which reality presents itself. Opposition to the requirement of reality in a novel is often based on a confusion of "reality" with the "ordinary" or the "sordid". To say that the novel must give us a sense of reality is not to say that the novelist's view of reality must conform to our view of it. On the contrary, one reason for reading novels is to enlarge one's view of reality by seeing what others consider real.[1] The ways in which a novel is "real" will be discussed in the chapter on criticism. Here it is necessary only to indicate the two kinds of unreality which distinguish other types of written prose fiction from the novel.

In my opinion the world portrayed in fiction must be a credible and possible one if the book is to be called a novel.[2] Many writers of fiction start with hypotheses contrary to fact: "if men went to Venus"; "if we lived in 1984"; "if all but a few people were killed by atomic blasts"; "if animals or insects talked"; "if a new island or country were discovered". Once we have accepted the hypothesis, we may find the presentation of the narrative realistic in its circumstantial detail and portrayal of human nature. Nevertheless, the hypothesis contrary to fact is basically different from the hypothesis of possibility with which the novelist starts.

Fantasy is itself a large category of prose fiction with a wide range of purpose and quality. Some fantasies are elementary forms of escapist literature with no value beyond the amusement of an idle hour. Others are designed for moral and theological indoctrination, like the fiction of C. S. Lewis or Charles

[1] Cf. Henry James, "The Art of Fiction", *The Future of the Novel*, ed. Leon Edel, Vintage Books, New York, 1956, p. 12.

[2] This book was written a year before I read Miss Mary McCarthy's article, "The Fact in Fiction", *Partisan Review*, XXVII (Summer, 1960), 438–58. The striking similarity in our opinions is welcome as corroborative evidence for their truth.

Williams. Still others are satires, like *Gulliver's Travels* and *Animal Farm*. Such fantasies may be real in the sense that the meaning communicated to us strikes us as true, but they are not real in the sense that we have an illusion that the action could have taken place as the writer says that it did.

Some fantasies are like allegories in that the author is more concerned with teaching or warning than he is with involving the reader in a world. To create a world is complicated. For instance, worlds have at least two dimensions – the natural and the human – and for many writers a third – the supernatural. The world contains many human beings, a few of whom we know very well, some well, many slightly, and the vast majority not at all. Actions happen simultaneously. Most human action is significant only to the individual, the daily round of eating, working, and sleeping. It is one of the major paradoxes of the novel that it attempts to convey the multiplicity and chaos of the actual world through words arranged in sentences.

In the actual world meaning must be found by each person. He has to seek within people and situations for their significance. No one wears a placard saying, "I'm faithful" or "I'm hypocrisy". We have the Springfield Fair and the Brussels Fair, but not Vanity Fair. In a novel the illusion of a world is achieved through inherent meaning. The characters are people with names like Pamela Andrews or Emma Woodhouse or Tom Jones. The places are Highbury and Frenchman's Bend if they are not Albany and London. The time is often stated exactly. The novel, like the actual world, is concerned with particular people at particular times and in particular places. This particularity contributes to the effect of reality.

Particularity also contributes to the distinctiveness of the novel as an art form. It is this particularity with its inherent meaning that distinguishes the novel from the fable. A fable is a written prose narrative, imagined and real, but not containing a world. In a fable the meaning is more basic than the illusion of a world. The characters are given special names, like Pilgrim and Hope, or they exemplify certain traits. They *mean* before they *are*. The actions are intended to prove a point. The narrative can be reduced to a logical exposition. *Pilgrim's Progress* is a good example of a fable. Bunyan, the teacher and preacher, is using vividly conceived characters to exemplify his meaning. His intent is not to show the reader the world as it is, but to move the reader into moral action. The image of a world was for him a means to an end, not the end itself.

If the novel involves the reader in an imagined real world, then narratives of fact, fantasies, and fables are not novels. Factual narratives include autobiographies, biographies, histories, and case studies. Fantasies are contrary to fact: narratives about talking animals, human visits to planets, future events, gods, ghosts, vampires, and other unnatural or supernatural beings. Fables of whatever form – allegory, satire, propaganda – are not novels.

NEW

No definition of the novel should ignore the name itself. The word means *new*. To qualify as a novel, fiction must in some sense be new. I think the newness comes from the new meaning of "original" which accompanied the changing attitudes of the eighteenth century. A novel is new if it originates in a direct vision of reality. A writer, to qualify as a novelist, must look for himself at the world he lives in; he must forge in the crucible of his imagination a new vision of a world. It is new if he saw it for himself; it is true if we accept it as a real world once our eyes have been opened to it. Once seen, a world can be quickly imitated. Great novelists have always been followed by imitators who think they can write good novels if they write like Jane Austen.

The newness is sometimes achieved in the choice of a setting of a philosophy of life or an area of human consciousness or a type of character. Each one may contribute something to the impression of novelty, but the novelty which is perennially fresh is the novelty of style. The great novelists are not necessarily the inventors or the experimenters; they are the men and women who can communicate their individuality through language. Their minds and attitudes shine through their words. Their personalities are felt by the reader.

In contrast to the novel, much fiction is composed in accordance with a formula. The detective story, the western, the love story, the success story, the adventure story are familiar types of fiction. Each type has a definite formula with strict conventions. Characters are good or bad, and the good characters always defeat the bad in the end. These types of fiction are various manifestations of the desire to escape reality. Circumstantial details may help to convey a plausible world of people and places, but conventions act as shock absorbers to divert our attention from the reality of feeling. For example, detective stories are full of murders, but no one really dies and is buried. We are protected from feeling grief because no character is truly grief-stricken; we are protected from feeling terror and guilt because the murderer gets what he deserves. The world portrayed is just credible enough in superficial ways to keep us reading, but not credible enough for us to succumb to any illusion that it is real. If it should create this illusion, it fails of its purpose to divert though it may achieve another end and become a novel.

Are these books poor novels because they fail to convey a deep sense of reality or good fiction because they achieve the intended goal of soothing troubled spirits and amusing the lonely and bored? My inclination is to say the latter. I would separate them from novels and call the whole genre of escapist fiction "romances" if the word *romance* had not acquired so many meanings in its long history. In particular, the controversy about romances and novels in the nineteenth century has made *romance* a special term in the criticism of fiction. Whatever we call them, the old, old stories of Cinderella and Jack the Giant-Killer dressed in the latest fashion for each generation serve useful functions, but they are not the same functions as the new stories of the novelists.

The newness of a *novel* is the newness of individual insight and the uniqueness of human personality. Such novelty has substance and depth; it never loses its brightness with passing time or closer acquaintance.

SUMMARY

The novel may be defined then as the form of written prose narrative of considerable length involving the reader in an imagined real world which is new because it has been created by the author. The converse of this statement is part of the definition: any form of literature which is oral, poetry, description, exposition, drama, short, fact, fantasy, fable, or formula is *not* a novel.

When we consider the full implications of this definition, we see what a formidable task the writing of a novel is. The formal problems of a long written prose narrative are difficult enough in themselves, but they are slight in comparison with the major problems of creating from the imagination a new world which will seem real to the reader. What is more, both sets of problems can be solved only in terms of the other. What the novelists themselves say about the nature of their work and their methods of solving the problems is the subject for the next chapter.

2 · What is a Novelist?

The question, What is a novelist? has been answered by implication in the definition of a novel. A novelist is a creator of a
world through words on paper. He imagines reality. He is
perennially new no matter how old.

How does he accomplish these apparently impossible tasks?
Curiously enough, he must first of all assume an unreal and
untrue rôle in the novel. If he does not, if he is honest and says
explicitly to the reader, "I am writing a story", he immediately destroys the illusion of reality he is trying to create.
Henry James comments on the rôle of the novelist in the
following highly significant passage:

> I was lately struck, in reading over many pages of
> Anthony Trollope, with his want of discretion in this par-
> ticular. In a digression, a parenthesis or an aside, he con-
> cedes to the reader that he and this trusting friend are only
> "making believe". He admits that the events he narrates
> have not really happened, and that he can give his narrative
> any turn the reader may like best. Such a betrayal of a
> sacred office seems to me, I confess, a terrible crime; it is
> what I mean by the attitude of apology, and it shocks me
> every whit as much in Trollope as it would have shocked
> me in Gibbon or Macaulay. It implies that the novelist is
> less occupied in looking for the truth (the truth, of course I
> mean, that he assumes, the premises that we grant him,
> whatever they may be) than the historian, and in doing so it
> deprives him at a stroke of all his standing room. To repre-
> sent and illustrate the past, the actions of men, is the task
> of either writer, and the only difference that I can see is, in
> proportion as he succeeds, to the honour of the novelist, con-

sisting as it does in his having more difficulty in collecting his evidence, which is so far from being purely literary. It seems to me to give him a great character, the fact that he has at once so much in common with the philosopher and the painter; this double analogy is a magnificent heritage.[1]

Any reader of novels by Henry James can see clearly how his concept of himself as historian, philosopher, and painter has affected the world he presents and the impact of that world on the reader.

The novelist as historian is a heritage from the eighteenth century, when novelists thought the illusion of reality could be achieved through the illusion of actuality. Henry Fielding in his first novel, *The History of the Adventures of Joseph Andrews*, repeatedly writes of himself as an historian. Even further removed from responsibility for words and action are Richardson and Defoe, who pretend they are editors of the letters or autobiographies of their characters.

Modern novelists, rebelling against the Victorian philosophers and historians who commented on their characters and situations, have withdrawn from the novel's surface completely. The classic statement of the modern novelist is the following sentence of Stephen Dedalus in James Joyce's *A Portrait of the Artist as a Young Man*:

> The artist, like the God of the creation, remains within or behind or beyond or above his handiwork, invisible, refined out of existence, indifferent, paring his fingernails.[2]

The truth is that any rôle assumed by the novelist in a novel is not his true rôle. The novelist is a novelist, *not* an editor, biographer, historian, philosopher, painter, or indifferent God. The assumed rôle is part of the technique by which the novelist achieves the effect he strives for. At present, the fashion favours the apparently non-existent author. Some people are now so accustomed to the current fashion that they dislike the rôles authors assumed in the past. They say that they like to

[1] "The Art of Fiction", p. 6. 　　[2] New York, 1956, p. 215.

interpret characters for themselves; they do not want to be told by the novelist what kind of people the characters are. They go so far as to assume that they have special insight into the characters not derived from the novelist. For example, one reader of *Middlemarch* told me that George Eliot was unfair to Rosamond because Rosamond was in actuality not infantine at all. What we need to keep always in mind is that the supposedly non-existent author of contemporary novels does in actuality exist. He pretends to be non-existent because that is the convention which now seems to us to create the illusion of reality, just as the contemporary dramatist pretends no audience is present at his play (unlike Shakespeare who gave his characters soliloquies and asides to address to the audience).

What, then, is the real nature of the novelist? To answer this question, I have turned to statements made by the novelists themselves. I have read journals, letters, prefaces, essays, and reports of interviews, and I have listened to lectures. All of them agree on the essentials, with the exception of one contemporary novelist who says he uses tricks.[1] The rest are fundamentally in agreement about the nature of their art, although they vary considerably in their conscious awareness of it, or rather, to be precise, they vary in the degree of explicit articulation of their methods.

THE PROBLEM

The problem of the novelist has been succinctly stated by Joyce Cary:

> This is every writer's dilemma. Your form is your meaning, and your meaning dictates the form. But what you try to convey is reality – the fact plus the feeling, a total complex experience of a real world. If you make your scheme too explicit, the framework shows and the book dies. If you

[1] Angus Wilson, *Writers at Work, The Paris Review Interviews*, ed. Malcolm Cowley, New York, 1958, p. 257. "All fiction for me is a kind of magic and trickery – a confidence trick, trying to make people believe something is true that isn't."

hide it too thoroughly, the book has no meaning and therefore no form. It is a mess.[1]

"Your form is your meaning, and your meaning dictates the
form." This is a key sentence. Reader and critic need always
to keep in mind that the novelist is conveying reality *through*
design.

THE AIM

The aim of a novelist is the assimilation of meaning into form.
He is not preaching or teaching or "selling" an idea. His meaning is implicit in every word, in every character, action, and
description. The form in which reality is presented is the
meaning.

Erskine Caldwell said in an interview, "Well, there is a
meaning in every story. But whether I'm trying to sell that
idea is something else. I'm just trying to portray it, to tell the
story of it as I see it – in terms of the characters themselves."[2]
William Faulkner makes the same point:

> If the writer concentrates on what he does need to be in-
> terested in, which is the truth and the human heart, he
> won't have much time left for anything else, such as ideas
> and facts like the shape of noses or blood relationships,
> since in my opinion ideas and facts have very little con-
> nection with the truth.[3]

Virginia Woolf wrote:

> I believe that all novels, that is to say, deal with char-
> acter, and that it is to express character – not to preach
> doctrines, sing songs, or to celebrate the glories of the
> British Empire – that the form of the novel, so clumsy,

[1] *Writers at Work*, p. 55. Cf. Henry James, *The Art of the Novel*, ed.
Richard P. Blackmur, New York, 1934, p. 14; David Cecil, *The Fine
Art of Reading and Other Literary Studies*, London, 1957, p. 95.
[2] Carvel Collins, "Erskine Caldwell at Work", *The Atlantic 202* (July,
1958) 22.
[3] *Writers at Work*, p. 138.

verbose, and undramatic, so rich, elastic, and alive, has been evolved.[1]

The conclusion to be drawn from this is that we should seek in a novel for a presentation of the world as it is, not as it ought to be or ought not to be. That readers of novels do learn from an awareness of an imagined real world, and that they may alter their conduct as a result of this awareness is another point. We may learn from those who are not teachers. But, in looking for the lesson or the message, we may miss the meaning, because the novelist aimed at meaning inherent in the imagined real world and not at a lesson illustrated by a story.

THE STARTING POINT

The starting point seems to be simple and single. These two words are often used by novelists to describe the germ or nucleus of their novels. Miss May Sarton in a lecture stressed the simplicity of the flash of insight which heralds a novel.[2] It may be an image, a feeling, a scrap of conversation. A novelist has an epiphany, to borrow Joyce's term, a revelation which, like a seed, may be lost to sight when the flower has bloomed. Four novelists are quoted below as illustrations of their agreement on this point. The italics are mine.

> It was years ago, I remember, one Christmas Eve when I was dining with friends: a lady beside me made in the course of talk one of those allusions that I have always found myself recognizing on the spot as "germs". The germ, wherever gathered, has ever been for me the germ of a "story", and most of the stories straining to shape under my hand have sprung from *a single small* seed, a seed as minute and wind-blown as that casual hint for "The Spoils of Poynton" dropped unwittingly by my neighbour, a mere floating particle in the stream of talk.[3]

[1] *Mr. Bennett and Mrs. Brown*, 2nd ed., London, 1928, pp. 9–10.
[2] "The Design of the Novel", The Sophie C. Hart Lecture, delivered at Wellesley College, November 12, 1958.
[3] James, *The Art of the Novel*, p. 119.

With me, a story usually begins with a *single* idea or memory or mental picture. The writing of the story is simply a matter of working up to *that moment*, to explain why it happened or what it caused to follow.[1]

And the beginning will be always the same; it is almost a geometrical problem: I have such a man, such a woman, in such surroundings. What can happen to them to oblige them to go to their limit? That's the question. It will be sometimes *a very simple incident*, anything which will change their lives.[2]

Actually I only have *one idea* at a time. It may be a very *small* idea that you can express in ten words. I start from that, I suppose, and see what happens.[3]

TRANSFORMATION

The transformation of the actual into an imagined reality is the function of the imagination. What happens between the observation of actual people and the creation of characters is a mystery which cannot be explained to those who have not experienced it. All that can be said is that *something does happen*. A character is not a portrait of an actual person, although he may resemble in many respects an actual person. He gives an illusion of reality because he is unique. Like actual people who resemble other actual people but are each one unique, so characters in novels resemble actual people but are each one unique if they are to seem real.

The passages below are quoted from four novelists:

Mauriac: There is almost always a real person in the beginning, but then he changes so that sometimes he no longer bears the slightest resemblance to the original. In general it is only the secondary characters who are taken directly from life.

Interviewer: Have you a special system for changing a real person into an imaginary one?

[1] William Faulkner, *Writers at Work*, p. 133.
[2] Georges Simenon, Ibid., p. 151.
[3] Erskine Caldwell, *The Atlantic 202* (July 1958), p. 22.

Mauriac: There is no system . . . it is simply the art of the novel. What takes place is a sort of crystallization around the person. It is quite indescribable. For a true novelist this transformation is a part of one's inner life. If I used some trick of prefabrication the result would not be a living character.[1]

We all like to pretend we don't use real people, but one does actually. . . . A useful trick is to look back upon such a person with half-closed eyes, fully describing certain characteristics. I am left with about two-thirds of a human being and can get to work. A likeness isn't aimed at and couldn't be obtained, because a man's only himself amidst the particular circumstances of his life and not amid other circumstances.[2]

As I have said, my conviction is that all serious creative work must be at bottom autobiographical, and that a man must use the material and experience of his own life if he is to create anything that has substantial value. But I also believe now that the young writer is often led through inexperience to a use of the materials of life which are, perhaps, somewhat too naked and direct for the purpose of a work of art. The thing a young writer is likely to do is to confuse the limits between actuality and reality. He tends unconsciously to describe an event in such a way because it actually happened that way, and from an artistic point of view I can now see that this is wrong. . . . Everything in a work of art is changed and transfigured by the personality of the artist.[3]

The life of the imagination will always remain separated from the life of reality. It feeds upon the life of reality, but it is not that life – cannot be. Mr John Marin painting "Brooklyn Bridge", Henry Fielding writing *Tom Jones*, are not trying in the painting and the novel to give us reality. They are striving for a realization of something out of their

[1] Francois Mauriac, *Writers at Work*, p. 43.

[2] E. M. Forster, Ibid., p. 32.

[3] Thomas Wolfe, *The Story of a Novel*, New York, 1949, pp. 21–2.

own imaginative experience, fed to be sure upon the life immediately about. A quite different matter from making an actual picture of what they see before them.[1]

The best way to understand the creative process is, of course, to write a novel oneself. The next best way is to observe it at secondhand by living with a novelist and following the writing of a novel step by step. This secondhand position is well represented by Stanislaus Joyce.

> These incidents, trivial as they are and such as might happen to any boy, suffice to show that my brother was not the weak, shrinking infant who figures in *A Portrait of the Artist*. He has drawn, it is true, very largely upon his own life and his own experience, and the vividness of his early impressions is due in great part, no doubt, to the fact that at college he suddenly found himself among boys bigger and older but less intelligent than himself. But *A Portrait of the Artist* is not an autobiography; it is an artistic creation. . . . As the other characters are often blends of real persons fused in the mould of the imagination, so for the character of Stephen in both drafts of the novel he has followed his own development closely, been his own model, and chosen to use many incidents from his own experience, but he has transformed and invented many others.[2]

Since most of us are unable either to write novels or to live with novelists, our only recourse is to study the creative process at thirdhand. I recommend, for example, studying the changes made by Joyce in *Stephen Hero* as one step towards producing *A Portrait of the Artist*. A comparison of Stephen Dedalus with James Joyce as he is revealed in his letters, in the reminiscences of his relatives and friends, and in biographies will be an excellent way for anyone to see what happens to the actual when an artist transforms it by the power of his imagination into the real.

[1] Sherwood Anderson, "Man and His Imagination", *The Intent of the Artist*, ed. Augusto Centeno, Princeton, New Jersey, 1941, p. 67.
[2] *My Brother's Keeper*, New York, 1958, p. 17.

EXPLORATION

Novelists have said that they work slowly through a novel, feeling their way as they go. They do not have a plot thoroughly worked out in detail before they begin. Rather they start from a point and explore or they have a destination in view but they are not clear about the landmarks on the way. Miss Sarton emphasized this point in her lecture, "The Design of the Novel", delivered at Wellesley College. Theme and characters, she said, precede plot. I shall quote from only two other novelists to illustrate this point, but additional novelists could be cited.

> The novelist should, I think, always settle when he starts what is going to happen, what his major event is to be. He may alter this event as he approaches it, indeed he probably will, indeed he probably had better, or the novel becomes tied up and tight. But the sense of a solid mass ahead, a mountain round or over or through which . . . the story must somehow go, is most valuable and, for the novels I've tried to write, essential. . . . When I began *A Passage to India* I knew that something important happened in the Malabar Caves, and that it would have a central place in the novel – but I didn't know what it would be.[1]

For the truth is that the work of art as completely realized is the result of a long and complex process of exploration, as well as construction. This is true even of a painter. The notion that a painter suddenly imagines a composition expressive of his feeling and straightway puts it down, is untrue. He begins with a general idea, no doubt – if he has a landscape before his eyes, he wants to express his feeling about that landscape in colour and form. But he has not yet got colour and form on canvas, he has not translated the actual fields and trees into symbols and, however experienced he is, he does not know exactly how to get the effect he wants, or even if it is possible within the limits of his material. He proceeds by trial and error. Watch him at

[1] Forster, *Writers at Work*, pp. 26-7.

work. He is not only uncertain of the exact effect of separate touches, he is still more uncertain of the result of their contrast and conjunction. And the more experienced he is, the more accomplished and subtle, the more care he will take. Manet would scrape off his paint day after day until, after fifty trials, he could satisfy himself that no further improvement was possible. That is, he was not merely expressing an intuition, he was continually discovering new possibilities in his own work, now become objective to him, and realizing them. The whole process was one of exploration as well as expression.

This is true of all the arts. Poets gradually construct both their verse and their meaning by continued test and alteration; novelists discover new aspects of their theme, and also new limitations of their technique, as they work.[1]

CONSTRUCTION

Related to the exploration of meaning-through-design, is the construction of a novel as a work of art. Henry James is the foremost spokesman of the constructive art, but other novelists are conscious also of a compositional centre which determines selection, focus, and perspective. Themes, characters, incidents, places, point of view, language take their place in relation to this compositional centre. Henry James describes the process of construction as follows:

That points, I think, to a large part of the very source of interest for the artist: it resides in the strong consciousness of his seeing all for himself. He has to borrow his motive, which is certainly half the battle; and this motive is his ground, his site and his foundation. But after that he only lends and gives, only builds and piles high, lays together the blocks quarried in the deeps of his imagination and on his personal premises. He thus remains all the while in intimate commerce with his motive, and can say to himself – what really more than anything else inflames and sustains him –

[1] Joyce Cary, *Art and Reality*, New York, 1958, pp. 86–7.

that he alone has the *secret* of the particular case, he alone can measure the truth of the direction to be taken by his developed data.[1]

In his preface to *The Portrait of a Lady*, James illustrates this construction by writing of the centre he chose:

> "Place the centre of the subject in the young woman's own consciousness," I said to myself, "and you get as interesting and as beautiful a difficulty as you could wish. Stick to *that* – for the centre; put the heaviest weight into *that* scale, which will be so largely the scale of her relation to herself. . . . Place meanwhile in the other scale the lighter weight (which is usually the one that tips the balance of interest): press least hard, in short, on the consciousness of your heroine's satellites, especially the male; make it an interest contributive only to the greater one.[2]

As a consequence of this choice of a centre, *The Portrait of a Lady* has a good design.

> So far I reasoned, and it took nothing less than that technical rigour, I now easily see, to inspire me with the right confidence for erecting on such a plot of ground the neat and careful and proportioned pile of bricks that arches over it and that was thus to form, constructionally speaking, a literary monument. Such is the aspect that today *The Portrait* wears for me: a structure reared with an "architectural" competence. . . . On one thing I was determined; that, though I should clearly have to pile brick upon brick for the creation of an interest, I would leave no pretext for saying that anything is out of line, scale or perspective.[3]

CHOOSING WORDS

Only a few novelists comment on the problems involved in recording their vision in words on paper. It is, I think, signifi-

---

[1] *The Art of the Novel*, pp. 122–3.   [2] Ibid., p. 51.
[3] James, *The Art of the Novel*, p. 52.

cant that the classic statement about a novelist's use of language was made by a novelist whose native language was Polish, not English. Joseph Conrad wrote in his preface to *The Nigger of the Narcissus* the following:

> And it is only through complete, unswerving devotion to the perfect blending of form and substance; it is only through an unremitting never-discouraged care for the shape and ring of sentences that an approach can be made to plasticity, to colour, and that the light of magic suggestiveness may be brought to play for an evanescent instant over the commonplace surface of words: of the old, old words, worn thin, defaced by ages of careless usage.[1]

The most effective way to realize what "unswerving devotion" and "unremitting never-discouraged care" mean is to compare first drafts and early editions with the final edition of a novel. For the full effect one should do this for oneself; but, if the time and opportunity are lacking, reading the comparisons made by others can be illuminating. I recommend two good studies of revision: F. O. Matthiessen, "The Painter's Sponge and Varnish Bottle", Henry James, *The Major Phase*, New York, 1944, pp. 152–86; and Herbert Davis, "*Women in Love:* A Corrected Typescript", *University of Toronto Quarterly* XVII (October 1957), pp. 34–53.

WHAT A NOVELIST IS NOT

If the novelist is a transformer, an explorer, a builder, and a farmer, as the metaphors they use about writing suggest, then they are not magicians, foundry workers, mechanics, puppeteers, ventriloquists. These five misconceptions of the art of the novelist are so widely held and so misleading to readers that they need to be examined.

A metaphor commonly applied to a novelist is that he holds a mirror up to nature. One implication of this metaphor is that the novelist is a magician who creates an illusion by mechanical means and not by art. Another implication is that the

---

[1] Garden City, New York, 1926, p. xiii.

writer observed in the actual world people and places and tried in words to record his observations. The metaphor fails to take into account the very act of creation, to say nothing of the acts of selection and phrasing.

The metaphor of the foundry worker is implied in the use of the word "mould". Some people state or imply that a novelist has a mould into which he pours a content. Henry James encountered this misconception of the art of the novelist and attacked it in the following passage:

> Many people speak of it as a factitious, artificial form, a product of ingenuity, the business of which it is to alter and arrange the things that surround us, to translate them into conventional, traditional moulds. This, however, is a view of the matter which carries us but a very short way, condemns the art to an eternal repetition of a few familiar *clichés*, cuts short its development, and leads us straight up to a dead wall. Catching the very note and trick, the strange irregular rhythm of life, that is the attempt whose strenuous force keeps Fiction upon her feet.[1]

The parts of a novel which the novelist has contrived rather than created are dead machinery. They rattle incongruously and destroy the illusion of a real world. Mr Forster recognizes the distinction between contrivance and creation. He said in an interview, "I didn't know how to get Helen to Howards End. That part is all contrived."[2]

If the novelist seems to be a puppeteer pulling the strings of his puppets, then he is not a good novelist. The novelist must create the illusion that his characters are made of flesh and blood with wills of their own, and not made of wood and wire with strings attached. We can have no sense of an imagined real world unless the characters seem to us like people.

The ventriloquist is, like the puppeteer, a manipulator of dummies. If a character seems to be speaking out of character by voicing opinions we recognize as the author's, then he is not

[1] "The Art of Fiction", pp. 19–20.
[2] *Writers at Work*, p. 28.

a good character and the novelist is not a good novelist. A
good novelist creates characters who speak for themselves in
accordance with their own personalities and desires.

THE NOVELIST'S CONSCIOUSNESS

At this point the question is bound to arise, "Is a novelist conscious when he writes?" The question by its very nature for-
bids an answer. Novelists are too busy writing to observe
what they are conscious of as they write. After the work is
done, few novelists remember what they were conscious of and
what they were not. Those who do remember their states of
mind rarely consider it important to tell the public what those
states were. The result is that we can never know much about
any author's consciousness, and about many authors we may
know nothing. Glimpses are revealed through interviews,
journals, lectures, and letters. It is fascinating, for example, to
read Virginia Woolf's *A Writer's Diary* in conjunction with the
criticism of her novels. Nevertheless, at best our information
is meagre, fragmentary, and possibly unreliable because un-
verifiable. Edgar Allen Poe has told us exactly how he composed "The Raven", a method so bizarre that critics refuse to
accept his word. Yet, if Poe did not report honestly his state
of mind, what proof can be adduced of his dishonesty?

How important is this question of consciousness? To me it
is an interesting question. I am always curious to know the
answer for each novel and author. Sometimes, too, the answer
is reassuring. It is good to know, for example, that Mr Forster
himself realized the flimsiness of his contrivance in getting
Helen to Howards End. He has said, "People will not realize
how little conscious one is of these things; how one flounders
about."[1] Like the critics of Poe, I wonder about this. The
glimpses I have had into the consciousness of novelists have
convinced me that they are very much more conscious of what
they are doing than I am. The prefaces of Henry James, for
instance, open up vista after vista of depths of awareness often
too distant for my short-sighted vision to perceive clearly.

[1] *Writers at Work*, p. 34.

The very act of selection means that the novelist must constantly have rejected alternatives unknown to me. He was conscious of all his unsuccessful trials, while I am aware only of the published version.

The question interests me, and the answer is often illuminating, but to me it seems no more important than that. What is in the work is in the work whether the novelist was conscious when he wrote or only semi-conscious. In fact, the subconscious may be the source of the best parts of the novel. The critic should be concerned with his own awareness, not that of the novelist, and the test of the sensitivity of his awareness is the text of the novel, not the comments about the novel made by the novelist. The question of the novelist's awareness is ancillary rather than fundamental. To pursue the answer is a digression from the main direction of a critic's energy; if pursued too far, the critic may lose sight of his true aim.

What is the true aim? Mr Faulkner has said, "The artist is of no importance. Only what he creates is important. . . ."[1] In contrast, Henry James has said, "There is one point at which the moral sense and the artistic sense lie very near together; that is in the light of the very obvious truth that the deepest quality of a work of art will always be the quality of the mind of the producer."[2] It is one more paradox of the novel that both Mr Faulkner and Henry James are right: the artist is both of no importance and all important. This paradox, however, does not help to solve the problem of the critic's aim.

COMMUNICATION

The aim may be clarified if we consider one function of the novelist rarely stated explicitly because it is implicit in the act of publication. The novelist writes to be read. He rarely states this intention, but is no less important for being implicit. I am not suggesting that novelists necessarily write to make money through the sale of the novels (although some do) nor that they pander to low tastes (although some do). All I am stressing is

---

[1] *Writers at Work*, p. 123.   [2] "The Art of Fiction", p. 26.

that a novelist communicates to a reader. Joyce Cary speaks of this aspect of a novelist's task:

> The struggle to be read, the hatred which his work excited when it was published at last, embittered Lawrence. And this is the common case of the original artist. He wants not only to express his unique idea of things, but to communicate it.[1]

The fullest statement of this need of the novelist which I have read has been made by Bettina Linn, who was a novelist and Associate Professor of English at Bryn Mawr College, U. S. A.

> The second problem is different. It is the reader, it is yourselves. The writer must think of you as well as his characters. He must often say to himself: Remember, the reader wasn't there! He was not present at the scene of action in the story. But he must be made to see it. The reader also has his ideas about human nature and society, and they may be much better than the novelist's ideas. But our job is to make you believe, if only for a few hours, in our people and their world. An act of imaginative co-operation between reader and novel is needed. That is what we ask of you.[2]

"An act of imaginative co-operation between reader and novel is needed." The precise nature of this act is the subject for the next chapter.

[1] *Art and Reality*, pp. 90–1.
[2] "Fiction, Shorthand to Man's Shared Experience", *Bryn Mawr Alumnae Bulletin* 7 (Summer 1958).

3 · What is a Reader of Novels?

The answer to this question is paradoxical: the reader is himself a novelist. Through his imagination he re-creates the imagined real world darkly shadowed forth by the black words on the white page. This point has been succinctly stated by Percy Lubbock in *The Craft of Fiction:*

> The reader of a novel – by which I mean the critical reader – is himself a novelist; he is the maker of a book which may or may not please his taste when it is finished, but of a book for which he must take his own share of the responsibility. The author does his part, but he cannot transfer his book like a bubble into the brain of the critic; he cannot make sure that the critic will possess his work. The reader must therefore become, for his part, a novelist, never permitting himself to suppose that the creation of the book is solely the affair of the author.[1]

The creative art of reading a novel is discussed at some length by Mr Gordon Hall Gerould in what I consider one of the best books about the novel I have read, *How to Read Fiction.* Two sentences are quoted here for emphasis, but the whole book should be read by everyone seriously interested in the art of the novel.

> In a very real sense, the novel or romance does not exist except as the reader does his part and completes the transaction. . . . In other words, if we cannot or do not reconstruct a story in our own minds on the basis of the hints of the author, we are not reading it at all: we are merely reading about it.[2]

[1] Compass Books, New York, 1957, p. 17.
[2] Princeton, New Jersey, 1937, p. 110.

The reader is not, of course, a novelist in the same sense of the word an author is. The process of writing a novel described in the last chapter cannot simply be transferred to the reader. For one thing, the starting points of writer and reader are obviously poles apart: the writer starts with an image, an incident, a flash of insight; the reader starts with the first page of a book. For help in understanding the art of reading novels, I turn again to Joyce Cary's provocative study, *Art and Reality*:

> Reading is a creative art, subject to the same rules, the same limitations as the imaginative process by which any observer of the arts turns a mere lump of stone, colours scattered on a canvas, noise, things completely meaningless in themselves, into a formal impression. The meaning received is created by the imagination from the symbols, and that imagination must first be educated – as the artist himself was educated – in the use and meaning of a symbolic system. The reader may believe that he is completely receptive and uncritical, he may and should attempt to expose himself to an experience without prejudice, but in fact he is performing a highly active and complex creative act. The reason he does not notice it is because most of it takes place in the subconscious.[1]

Let us consider first the receptive mind, the exposure to an experience without prejudice, and then the nature of the "highly active and complex creative act".

RECEPTIVITY

We all have tastes and predilections: we naturally like some kinds of novels and dislike others. The list below cites some preferences I have noted in myself or in others. You may be able to add to the list. What is important is the recognition of these preferences and the willingness to keep these preferences in their proper place. We should not allow them to prevent our

---

[1] Pp. 119–20.

reading some novels with enjoyment and understanding, since one aim of reading novels is to widen our scope of appreciation and gain insight into worlds different from our own.

Place: Some people like to read only about the United States; others prefer novels set in England, Asia, Africa, South America, Australia, or even places like the Arctic or Easter Islands. People may like or dislike to read novels about life in hospitals, on ships, on farms, in small towns, in big cities.

Time: Some people prefer novels about the present; others prefer novels about the past.

Characters: People may like or dislike characters drawn from the aristocracy, the middle classes, or the workers, drawn from the very wealthy, the moderately well-to-do, or the poor, drawn from certain professions. They may like or dislike good characters or bad characters, healthy or sick, normal or abnormal.

Action: People may like or dislike lively action, violence, mystery, quiet everyday occurrences, happy endings.

Technique: People may like or dislike novels told in the first person or the third, with flashbacks, in letters.

Rôle of the Author: People may like or dislike a novel in which the author is audibly present, or explicitly describes the characters, or is apparently non-existent.

Point of View of the Reader: Some people like to identify themselves with one of the characters and to live the novel vicariously; others like to observe the world of the novel from a distance.

GOOD READING

If we start reading with an open mind and if the novel is good, we soon find ourselves reading creatively. The first sign of creative reading is that we lose ourselves in the imagined world. The actual world fades away from our consciousness. A good reader with a good book can be so lost to actuality that he does not hear bells ring, or smell food burn, or see shadows fall, or feel the tug of a child's hand. Everything else is forgotten because he is lost in the world of the novel.

Once in the world of the novel, the good reader lives in it. He re-creates the vision of the artist. As Joyce Cary wrote, "In this highly complex process, not only the creative imagination, the sympathies, the critical taste, are brought into play, but also knowledge of all kinds, of fact as well as art, of actuality as well as books."[1] Separating the imagination, the emotions, and the intellect as three parts of this complex process may suggest a division which in fact does not exist. A good reader responds instantaneously with the subtlety and complexity the words evoke. If in the next three paragraphs I write about the three faculties separately, I do so because each one is complicated enough in itself to need a paragraph. I do not intend to imply a tripartite psychology.

The imagination re-creates the world of the senses. We can see the hills, the woods, the moors, the houses, the rooms. We see the shapes and colours and distances of the physical world. The people also take shape in our minds. We see them walk and gesture; we note the colour of hair and eyes and complexion. Sounds, too, are re-created. We hear the distinctive voices of the people and the human sounds of city and country. We also hear the cries of birds and animals and the sounds of nature – the wind in the trees, the water in the brook, the thunder in the sky. The physical world is full of objects to be touched and smelled and tasted. We touch a loved-one's hair, a velvet drapery, a silk stocking. We smell the sea or the roses. We taste the cold tea or the roast turkey. Wherever the writer appeals to our senses. a good reader responds by imagining what it is like to walk through an English field in June or to hunt in the Spanish mountains or eat lunch in the cabin of a Negro in Mississippi.

The emotional response of the reader to the people and their actions may be conditioned by their physical appearance and by the sensuous impression of their environment. If the novel is good and the reader is responsive, his emotions will be complex and changing. Each new episode will reveal aspects of the characters which will evoke varied and changing feelings. The

[1] *Art and Reality*, p. 125.

reader may at once admire and detest a character, like and dislike at the same time. He may come to change completely his first feelings or he may keep the same feelings but be more fully aware of their implications. He may sympathize for different reasons with contending characters and thus feel within his mind the tensions and irreconcilable conflicts objectified in different characters.

A good reader of a good novel thinks as he reads. He observes the relationships of the inner lives of the characters to their outer lives. He remembers earlier speeches, actions, and attitudes and traces their consequences as the novel progresses. He anticipates the future and watches to see if his anticipation is fulfilled. He wonders if the characters and the novelist mean what they on the surface say. He probes beneath the surface and interprets the meaning of ambiguous remarks.

When a good reader enters the world of a novel, he enters with his whole attention and responds to everything in that world as if he were there. This does not mean that he loses his individuality. He brings with him his knowledge and ideas, his sympathies and antipathies. They play a part in his participation in the imagined world just as they play a part in his participation in the actual world. The difference – and oh what a blessed difference! – between the imagined world and the actual world is that characters cannot react to us, whereas people do. The characters are always beyond our reach; we can neither harm nor help them. We live vicariously in a world in which nothing is demanded of us and for which we bear no responsibility. No wonder so many people find the reading of novels one of life's greatest pleasures.

The novelist himself partly determines the way we read his novel. By his technique he places his reader at a certain point from which he views the story. This is called the point of view, and this point of view determines the aesthetic distance. At one extreme is the point of view of the consciousness of one character. Here the distance is so short that many readers say they "identify" themselves with the character. The next remove is listening to an "I" tell his own story. Our natural inclination to think that"I" means "me" leads again with some readers to identification. The distance, however, is beginning to broaden. When the point of view is that of one character, but the story is told in the third person, the distance again widens. If the point of view shifts from character to character, we need to stand farther away from them to see them all. The author may explicitly place his story in the past and at a distance. We then stand with him and look back at some long, completed action. The awareness of the point of view and the proper distance is an essential part of good criticism of a novel.

BAD READING

Good reading, as we have seen, is creative and responsive. Bad reading may be bad for a number of different reasons.

The reader may be called a novelist, but the novel he is composing is a re-creation and not a creation. If the reader wants to invent characters and situations he is free to do so, of course, but he should distinguish between the novel he re-creates and the novel he wants to write for himself. Some people with lively imaginations let them run wild. They add all sorts of episodes for which no hint exists in the novel. This is fun, but dangerous. It is very easy to lose sight of the original text of the novel and to read into the novel what has no place there.

Conversely, the reader once admitted to the novelist's world has an obligation to see as much as he can while he is there. A hasty visit of a hop, skip, and jump is as valueless as a three-week jaunt to Europe with stop-overs in five countries. Every word in a novel has or should have a function. Skipping sections may totally distort the meaning of the novel.

Unwillingness to enter a world with an active imagination and responsive heart makes a poor reader. Some people are still brought up to distrust both the imagination and the emotions. If they read novels at all, they do so gingerly and unresponsively. One of these people told me she read novels for the nuggets of truth contained in them! To her the characters and dialogue and narrative were suspect because they might arouse emotion. Novels are fiction and they must be read as fiction. The reader who tries to read fiction as if it were non-fiction will miss the point as surely as he will if he tries to read non-fiction as if it were fiction. The person who wants to know before he starts to read a novel what he should "look for" is confusing fiction with non-fiction. A reader should not "look for" specific points in reading a novel; he should enter the imagined world and live through an experience.

Selective involvement is not quite so fatal as complete detachment, but it does distort the novel. A good reader accepts the novelist's premises. One of those premises is the point of view and the consequent distance. A good reader willingly accepts the point of view the novelist asks him to and looks at the world from the distance required. He does not insist on "identifying" with a character if identification is not called for; nor does he insist on standing aloof if a closer view is expected. A poor reader wants always to read from one point of view and from one distance, with the result that either he likes only a very few novels or he distorts some novels to suit his taste.

RE-READING NOVELS

Art offers us one advantage that life cannot: we can re-experience it. We can be sure that Elizabeth will marry Darcy when we pick up *Pride and Prejudice* for the second or fiftieth time. Novels offer us a stable world in the midst of the flux of actuality. They offer us repeated pleasure. They give us the opportunity to learn from experience and to bring that new insight to bear on the same experience. And with each re-reading of a good novel, we gain in appreciation and insight. A good novel needs and deserves re-reading; a bad novel cannot be re-read. Re-reading of a novel is thus a sound test of quality.

If the novel is good, we do not miss the suspense of not knowing what is to happen next. On the contrary, the tension created by our foreknowledge and inevitability of conclusion makes for more absorbing reading than simple curiosity. We know what is to take place, but the characters do not. If only we could warn them! "Oh, no!" "Don't do it." "Listen to him!" we inwardly respond. Yet we know that, given these people as they are, they cannot act differently. This frustration we feel contributes to the impression of reality the novel gives us because in actual life we often suffer the frustration of knowing an inevitable ending without being able to prevent it.

Re-reading a novel is likely to be more leisurely than the first reading. We are not hurried along by curiosity and thus have more inclination to observe details. These details now carry a significance we could not note at the time. For example, a first reading of *The Portrait of a Lady* could yield but a small portion of its meaning. What is the significance of Madame Merle's reference to the cup? What is the implication of Mr Touchett's bequest to Isabel? What does it mean to "see Europe" or "to live"? All the painful overtones of irony await the second reading. We never know until we have completed the novel what the full significance of every detail is.

Only when we do understand the significance of every detail, can we respond to the design of the novel. With each re-reading of a good novel, the relation of image to meaning emerges more and more clearly until we can experience the novel as a compositional whole. We can then feel the effects of the structure, of the relevance of the parts to the central theme, and of the meaning inherent in the image. The re-creation of the form of the novel is extremely difficult, because the novel as a whole exists only inside of the reader's imagination. Our perceptions of what is in the book are the materials for our reconstruction.

The structure of a novel is the relation between two orders: the numerical order of pages and the chronological order of action. A novel is a book and as a book it is composed of pages read in consecutive order. A novel is also a narrative of actions in time. The simplest structure for a novel is one where the two orders coincide. The earliest important action in the narrative is the first action in the book. Nothing that happened before this is important enough to be stressed later in the book. As we turn the pages, the actions follow each other chronologically. When we reach the last page, we end with the last significant action. So simple a structure is rarely found. Often the first chapter contains the middle or end of the action; often the last chapter is felt to be the middle with the end left to our imagination. Sometimes the structure is very complicated, with frequent shifts from past to future to present.

Related to our awareness of the chronological order is our awareness of simultaneous actions. On the page only one set of actions can be presented, yet all the characters in the imagined world are supposedly alive and active somewhere off the page. What the characters not on the stage, so to speak, are doing may very materially affect the characters who are on the stage. This off-stage action is the source of suspense for the reader. A second reading changes our response from surprise to awareness of the blindness and dangers of the characters. In a good novel the relation between the perceived action and the discovered action is a part of the significant and affective design.

Responding to the relations of the parts in the design is a very important aspect of reconstructing a novel. The difficulty here is that the parts of a novel are not like the parts of a machine – separate divisible entities. We cannot talk about characters, description, dialogue, incident, technique, and style as if each were a unit. Henry James has stated this point succinctly:

> People often talk of these things as if they had a kind of internecine distinctness, instead of melting into each other at every breath, and being intimately associated parts of one general effort of expression. I cannot imagine composition existing in a series of blocks, nor conceive, in any novel worth discussing at all, of a passage of description that is not in its intention narrative, a passage of dialogue that is not in its intention descriptive, a touch of truth of any sort that does not partake of the nature of incident, or an incident that derives its interest from any other source than the general and only source of the success of a work of art – that of being illustrative. A novel is a living thing, all one and continuous, like any other organism, and in proportion

as it lives will it be found, I think, that in each of the parts there is something of each of the other parts.[1]

If the novel is an organism, then its parts are functions. The functions operate in relation to the significant and effective design. Let us take one novel, *Great Expectations,* as an example. Divisions into such parts as characters, setting, dialogue, and action are arbitrary and false. The division in terms of the nature of the expectations, their "greatness", their thwarting, their fulfilment, is a sound and significant division. Miss Havisham cannot be separated into "character", "action", "dialogue", "setting". She and everything related to her function to produce in the reader the awareness of how thwarted expectation can turn good into evil. Each novel as a unique organism has unique parts. To become aware of a novel as a compositional whole is to become aware of what its parts *are* as well as how these parts are related.

Each individual no doubt becomes aware of a novel as a whole in slightly different ways. For some re-creating a novel is a strenuous activity calling for the exercise of imagination and memory, emotional response, and intellectual penetration. For others it may be a sudden revelation. Virginia Woolf describes as follows how she reads a novel:

> The first process, to receive impressions with the utmost understanding, is only half the process of reading; it must be completed, if we are to get the whole pleasure from a book, by another. We must pass judgement upon these multitudinous impressions; we must make of these fleeting shapes one that is hard and lasting. But not directly. Wait for the dust of reading to settle; for the conflict and the questioning to die down; walk, talk, pull the dead petals from a rose, or fall asleep. Then suddenly without our willing it, for it is thus that Nature undertakes these transitions, the book will return, but differently. It will float to the top of the mind as a whole. And the book as a whole is different from the book received currently in separate phrases. Details

[1] "The Art of Fiction", p. 15.

now fit themselves into their places. We see the shape from start to finish; it is a barn, a pig-sty, or a cathedral.[1]

Whatever our method, we need to learn how "to grasp the shadowy and fantasmal form of a book, to hold it fast, to turn it over and survey it at leisure" because "that is the effort of a critic of books . . ."[2] Let us now turn our attention to the critic of the novel.

[1] "How Should One Read a Book?" *The Second Common Reader*, New York, 1932, pp. 290–1.
[2] Lubbock, p. 1.

4 · What is a Critic of Novels?

The reading of novels and the criticism of novels are not two different activities although the two words – *reading* and *criticism* – give the impression that they are. Many people think that anyone can read a novel but that only a few highly selected and trained individuals with special gifts can criticize one. Reading and criticism are, however, one process. An aware reader is a critic. Since everyone is more or less aware of what he is reading and what he thinks of his reading, every reader is more or less a critic. A critic, then, is to my way of thinking not different from a reader in kind but in quality. Criticism is the articulation of the reader's experience. If you are aware of the intention of the novelist, of the nature of the novel, and of your experience in reading the novel and what evoked the experience, you are a critic. The quality of your awareness determines your quality as a critic.

While criticism so defined is a simple process in the sense of being familiar and natural, it is not simple in the sense of being easy or uncomplicated. Our experiences as we read are subtle, evanescent, and contradictory. We are aware of many things simultaneously, too many to put into words and some incapable of verbalization. Moreover, we cannot draw any clear line between what in the experience has been evoked by the novel and what we are reading into the novel because of the experiences we bring to our reading. The novel is by definition a long and complex literary form which makes new demands on a reader. The intention of the novelist is to imply through the evoked experience the meaning of his vision of life. He nowhere expressly states his meaning, nor can that meaning be reduced to a message.

A further complication is that the relations among these

factors are peculiar to literary criticism. They are non-sensory and therefore not easy to discern. Moreover, we have no adequate vocabulary to express these relations. The basic difficulty is that the link between novelist and critic is on an entirely different plane of reality from their minds. The novelist wants to communicate something to another through a vision of reality; the critic understands and evaluates that something through his re-creation of the vision. Here the terms are on the same plane: the imaginations, emotions, thoughts, and observations of human beings. But the link is a book: black marks in order on a white page.

The other arts hinder rather than help us with this problem of discerning the relations of novelist–novel–critic. The middle term in the arts *is* the vision; it *is* the image or sound to be apprehended. The artist paints the picture; the sculptor carves the statue. The analogy of a writer might be the composer who writes the score of his music, but the music and not the score is the art to be criticized. Yet when we talk about the novel we borrow the terms for relations which are spatial or temporal: pattern, design, vision, dimension, form, rhythm, tone.[1]

Another difficulty in writing about literary criticism is the uniqueness of individual experience. Every reading of every novel by each individual is a unique experience. If that uniqueness is lost sight of in generalizations or even specific statements about criticism, the main point is lost. The point is not what you should think when you read a novel; the point is what Katherine Lever did think when she read *Great Expectations* on February 10, 1959. Awareness is by its very nature of the moment. The moment gives it intensity and vitality. That the moment goes and can never be fixed is essential and not to be deplored. The point is that by being aware of our experiences *now* the change in awareness can be one of growing sensitivity, scope, and depth.

[1] Cf. Forster, *Aspects of the Novel*, p. 137, and Lubbock, *The Craft of Fiction*, pp. 10–11.

THE STARTING POINT

The starting point of criticism is the experience of the reader. "Would it not be more logical," you may ask, "to begin with the intention of the novelist? Is not *his* aim the starting point of the novel and thus of the critic?" The answer to this question is both "no" and "yes". I say "no" because the intention of the novelist cannot be solid ground for a critic. We do not know for certain precisely the intention of a particular novelist in a novel. We can reach inductively towards it, but we never can have the certainty that breeds confidence. The intention is not stated in the novel. Moreover, even if we read what a novelist wrote if he wrote about his novel, we still could not be certain. Our earlier study of the intentions of novelists must have made this clear.

This earlier study has also made clear that the fundamental intention of a novelist is, as Mr Forster says, "to bounce the reader into accepting what he says. . . ." [1] We *are* starting with the intention of the novelist when we start with the experience of the reader. The following quotations from two novelists will emphasize the soundness of this critical approach:

> The reader it is to be hoped will not give a thought to the book's method or to the book's lack of method. He is concerned only with the effect of the book as a whole on his mind. Of that most important question he is a far better judge than the writer. Indeed, given time and liberty to frame his own opinion he is eventually an infallible judge. [2]

> Nothing, of course, will ever take the place of the good old fashion of "liking" a work of art or not liking it: the most improved criticism will not abolish that primitive, that ultimate test. [3]

> To criticize is to appreciate, to appropriate, to take

[1] *Aspects of the Novel*, p. 75.

[2] Virginia Woolf, Introduction to *Mrs Dalloway*, Modern Library, New York, 1928, p. viii.

[3] James, "The Art of Fiction", p. 18.

intellectual possession, to establish in fine a relation with the criticized thing and make it one's own.[1]

A reader should be aware of the source of his response to a novel because through that awareness he can distinguish between novels that seem good for ephemeral reasons and those which are good for enduring reasons. All of us bring to our reading a multiplicity of associations and emotional desires. A novelist knows this and works with them to create his effects. If, however, a novel is designed to have an effect only upon what the reader brings to the novel, it will be necessarily limited. The best-sellers of a year or a decade ago or of another country illustrate graphically how a novel can seem good to thousands of readers because of what they bring to it, while the novel itself has so little to give that it cannot live long nor bear transplanting.

Every year novels on controversial subjects are published: inter-racial marriage, anti-Semitism, migrant workers, Communists. Our interest in the subject may be projected into the novel so that we consider the novel "interesting" and like it. The strength of our feelings on the subject may give life to paper characters. When our interest dies and our feelings subside, we can read the novel again and see it for what it is. Mrs Humphry Ward's *Robert Elsmere*, 1888, is an example of a novel which stirred interest with a controversial subject – religious doubt – but now fails to stir interest as a novel.

Controversial subjects are the most obvious sources of interest originating in the reader. Less obvious but still important are the associations readers have with familiar places, worlds, and types of characters. The recognition of cities or countryside imparts to a novel a reality which is adventitious. The pleasure of recognition can extend to a world as well as to an actual place. Family life can seem real if the man shaves and the woman puts her hair up in curlers and the children pick their noses and they all eat hamburgers and go to the toilet. "Just like life", we may respond, with the cosy feeling that

[1] James, Preface to *What Maisie Knew*, p. 155.

the daily round and common task have been dignified by having been recorded in print. Hospitals, schools, colleges, parishes, and business firms are microcosms familiar to many. Certain types of characters emerge at different times as particularly significant. Novels about these types are then especially interesting to many. *Babbitt* and *The Man in the Gray Flannel Suit* are two examples. Some years the type is the lovable adolescent and sometimes the unlovable, mixed-up kid; at other times the sensitive child is the fashion or the angry young man.

Novels which capitalize on current fashions in subjects, places, worlds, and types may or may not be good novels. The test question to ask is, "How much of my interest is engendered by the art of the novel and how much by my own associations and attitudes?" If the source is in me and the times, then the work may be good journalism but it is not a good novel.

By examining the source of our interest in and liking for a novel, we can also distinguish between novels and romances. In Chapter 1, I said a romance may be a good romance but a bad novel. The test for distinguishing the two is the source of our response. We all come to our reading of novels with desires. We are seeking or we would not be reading. If the fiction does no more than satisfy our desire for vicarious excitement, it is a romance. A romance is a trapdoor which enables us to escape from ourselves and our world for a few hours; a novel transports us into a new world and returns us to ourselves and our old-world with fresh insight.[1]

When we finish a work of fiction which held our interest and stirred our emotions, we should ask, "Did it satisfy desires already strong or did it enlarge my vision of the real?" I personally like romances. I like adventure which takes no toll

[1] The romance and the novel are not always defined in this way. Mr Richard Chase says, "Doubtless the main difference between the novel and the romance is in the way in which they view reality", *The American Novel and Its Tradition*, Doubleday Anchor Books, Garden City, New York, 1957, p. 12. The works he calls romances I would call novels because they do seek to render reality.

and glamorous love affairs without sordidness. I also long for a world where the good people are amusing, healthy, and successful and the wicked are punished. Clearly defined good and evil, just rewards, and happy endings satisfy my desire for a comprehensible, moral, and pleasant world. The reverse of this desire is equally romantic. Some people today like to believe that failure is success, that evil is good, that the ugly is beautiful. Their reversal of values finds satisfaction in fiction which reverses the values. In this fiction respectable men and women who earn a decent living through hard work, who are faithful in marriage and chaste if single, who worship God, and who contribute to their alma maters because they believe in a liberal arts education are at heart mean, vicious phonies incapable of love and generous selflessness. In contrast, the drug addicts, alcoholics, tramps, pimps, prostitutes, thieves, murderers, idiots, insane, liars, beggars, and perverts are at heart charitable and noble with tremendous depths of compassion and absolutely genuine sensitivity to the beauties of nature and art.

Fiction which satisfies our fantasies of the world as we wish it has its value. All I am saying here is that a good reader is aware that it is his fantasy which has been affected and not his imagination. A reader who makes this distinction can tell the difference between a good and a bad novel.

A novel as distinct from journalism and romance makes demands upon the reader. Mr Forster stresses this point:

> Our easiest approach to a definition of any aspect of fiction is always by considering the sort of demand it makes on the reader. Curiosity for the story, human feelings and a sense of value for the characters, intelligence and memory for the plot.[1]

To these aspects may be added the portrayal of the physical world which demands imagination. On another plane is the aspect of the author's technique which demands sensitivity to the nature and functions of language.

[1] *Aspects of the Novel*, p. 101.

These demands stretch our minds. We can feel the pulls when we read a good novel. Sometimes we are simultaneously pulled so hard in so many different directions that we cannot stand the strain for long at a time. Far from praising a novel because it is so enthralling we cannot put it down, we might rather consider higher praise that we felt it necessary to put the novel down frequently. Novelists with a genuinely new vision may make a new demand upon us which we are not prepared to tolerate. Mr Faulkner, for example, demands from his readers a willingness to endure being frustrated, outraged, helplessly and dumbly trapped, amused by the macabre, and impressed by good-in-evil. The recognition that we do feel these conflicting and strong responses is the starting point for our criticism of the particular novel.

"But," you may object, "the experience of the reader is subjective. How can statements based on *your* experience have any validity or meaning for *me*? Are you not advocating an ego-centred relativism?" No. The experience of the reader is the starting point for criticism but neither the centre nor the end. Once I have determined that my response has been evoked by the novel, I next look in the novel to see what has evoked the experience. My awareness of my own experience leads me into a closer examination of the novel.

"But you are still talking of your awareness. I always thought I should be objective. Shouldn't a critic establish in advance reasonable and impartial criteria by which to judge whether a novel is good or bad?" This is an opinion so widely held by intelligent people that it deserves thoughtful consideration. It appeals to our sense of justice and of scientific method. The trouble with this procedure is that, while it is appropriate for law courts and perhaps for a scientific laboratory, it is not appropriate for literary criticism. A critic should not be "objective" in the sense of not being emotionally involved. The essence of reading is involvement. Moreover, a critic does not "judge" a novel to be good or bad; he becomes aware of its quality. This distinction is fundamental.

As for the criteria, who is to decide them? The main point of a novel is that it be new. If we have ready-made criteria by which to judge a novel, we may well find ourselves judging as bad a novel which is so new it is extremely good. A further danger is that we do not think through the criteria for ourselves based on our own reading but accept the criteria of another. Then we find that one teacher or critic has one set and another has another set. No criteria are universally valid. We are, therefore, back to our original position of individual choice.

The two worst drawbacks of criticism interpreted as judgement by criteria seem to me to be the promotion of dependence upon others and superficiality. The unquestioning acceptance of criteria and their application to every new novel stunt the individual's growth. He gains security only at the cost of flexibility. He sees what he has been taught to see and fails to see new values. It is superficial because it is superimposed on the natural method of reading. Criticism, as I define it, is a natural and continuous process. Criticism, as judgement by standards, shifts ground after the reading has been completed. Attention is turned from reader and novel to objective standards, the origins of which may not even be known, much less authoritative. And who is the author of rules for the novel?

One criterion everyone would agree upon, I believe, and that is the criterion of James: "The only obligation to which in advance we may hold a novel, without incurring the accusation of being arbitrary, is that it be interesting." [1]

REALITY AND THE NOVEL

What is interesting to me in a novel is its reality. I like a novel which draws me in from the start and gives me the illusion that this is a real world in which I am living. Ortega y Gasset has expressed exactly what I mean:

> The author must see to it that the reader is cut off from his real horizon and imprisoned in a small hermetically sealed universe – the inner realm of the novel. He must

[1] "The Art of Fiction", p. 9.

make a "villager" of him and interest him in the inhabitants of this realm. For, however admirable these may be, they cannot hold their own against the beings of flesh and bone who form the reader's daily surroundings and constantly claim his interest. To turn each reader into a temporal "provincial" is the great secret of the novelist.[1]

To be cut off from my own world and involved in another is interesting to me and pleasant.

What is it that makes an imagined world real to me? Is it correspondence to actuality? Not for me. The reason for this answer is that the actual world is not always real to me. Actuality and reality are not the same in the actual world, so that correspondence to actuality does not guarantee reality in fiction. I have been in places and positions in which I have not felt real. "Is this really me?" I have asked myself. The actuality has moved faster than my imagination and feelings. Similarly, the death of a relative or friend has for a long time seemed unreal to me. I knew the fact to be actual, but I could realize it as true only slowly over months.

Often, too, I have had difficulty in realizing what others think and feel as real. They communicate through intensity of voice how deeply they fear or love or hate. I know they actually feel a certain way about people or situations, but the feeling is so out of proportion to the cause as I observe it that I am puzzled and unsympathetic. This is particularly true of anxieties arising from loss of self-esteem in some alien world in which my self-esteem is not involved. It seems unrealistic for anyone to care what the villagers say when another's village is being observed. What people in our own village say about us is, of course, very important!

A further problem of realization is created by communication through writing. A foreign country is not *ipso facto* real to me just because the author of a travel book is stating actual facts. The way the facts are presented determines the degree to which the foreign country seems real to me. If the account is

[1] *Notes on the Novel,* p. 90.

vague, superficial, and poorly organized, I am not transported into another world. If the author's egotism constantly intrudes between me and the world described, I see him and not the world.

What makes actuality real to me? First of all, it must be imaginable. I believe what I can see, hear, taste, touch, smell for myself, if not in the flesh, then in the imagination. Sense impressions – vivid, clear sense impressions – help to convince me of the reality of what I read. Moreover, that we exist in the body means that each individual is unique and every event is unique. No two people are alike. Since each event occurs in time and place, no two events are identical. Vagueness, types, generalities, abstractions seem unreal to me because they are untrue to the particularities of existence.

Secondly, the actual becomes real when I feel it to be real. By an act of imagination I can be charitable towards others, but this is not the same as feeling what they feel. Love, hate, envy, anger, pity, jealousy, despair – these are real only when I feel them. Even emotions I myself have had in the past are difficult to recall, and emotions I have never felt in any degree cannot be real to me.

Thirdly, reality is confirmed by experience. When every tiny incident and detail becomes meaningful only in the light of one explanation, then the explanation is convincingly real. When I understand the motives of people and their relationships, they begin to exist for me. In other words, a particular of any kind becomes real through its place in a whole.

In fact, then, the real is complex. It embraces the actual and goes beyond it. What is contrary to actuality is not real to me. The instantaneous response, "But that's not true!" shatters any image of reality. But the converse is not true. The response, "That's a fact!" does not guarantee reality. Indeed, facts may clash with the imagined reality and shatter the illusion as completely as errors. The definition of *reality* in Webster's Fifth Collegiate Dictionary stresses both the meanings of "existent or actual" and the meaning of the "genuine", "true", "fundamental, and ultimate", "intrinsic and of the essence". The complexity of reality calls for both complexity in the novel and in the response evoked by the novel. If I am to call a novel real, my imagination and emotions must be so stimulated that I become involved in the imagined world at the same time that my intellect is convinced this imagined world is a true, fundamental, and ultimate world.

Before discussing what makes a novel real, I want to make clear what I mean when I say this imagined world is "real" to me. I do not mean that it is an actual world or an historical world. It is not an exclusively real world; other very different worlds may be equally real. Nor does it need to be real in all ways consistently throughout. Some worlds are more interesting because they convince me of their truth than because they move me deeply. Finally, I do not mean that the world is good or bad, pleasant or unpleasant. I *do* mean that I am interested in it; I am touched by it; and I am convinced of its truth.

THE IMAGINED WORLD

My first impulse in thinking of a world is to think of it as a geographical unit. Certainly geography is significant. The boundaries of many an imagined world are the boundaries of village or town with only occasional glimpses of a larger world beyond. The world of *Emma* is the world of Highbury with only one excursion to Donwell Abbey and one to Box Hill. Similarly the world of *The Hamlet* is almost entirely contained within Frenchman's Bend. In other novels – *Great Expectations*, for example – the village and the metropolis are contrasted. In still others the world of the novel includes cities of many nations. The action of *The Portrait of a Lady* takes place in Albany, London, Paris, Florence, and Rome as well as in the country homes of the Touchetts and Lord Warburton.

Through their bodies and bodily actions people form part of this dense web. Through their psyches the people form social worlds within the geographical worlds. An English village may be viewed from the top down as Jane Austen does in *Emma* or from the bottom up as Charles Dickens does in *Great Expectations*. The world of *Emma* goes down as far as the Martins, substantial farmers; the blacksmith does not exist for Jane Austen. The world of the village in *Great Expectations* is the world of the blacksmith; the gentry do not exist for Dickens. The presence of the eccentric Miss Havisham merely accentuates the absence of the normal upper classes. *Middlemarch* is the example *par excellence* of varied human worlds within one geographical world. Of the three heroines Dorothea Brooke is so removed from the others that she never encounters Mary Garth and only in one memorable scene crosses the path of Rosamund. The human worlds in *A Passage to India* are divided not only by class, wealth, education, and profession, but also by race and religion.

A Passage to India illustrates both the varying human worlds of English and Indian in the town of Chandrapore and the varying spiritual powers of the Anglican God, of Mohammed, of Shri Krishna, of the untouchable punkah wallah who was a god, and of the echo of the Marabar Caves. This novel is unusual in the diversity and strength of the spiritual powers depicted, but not unusual in the depiction of spiritual powers. The religious concerns of human beings naturally are represented in novels. Conflicting religious beliefs and practices must necessarily play a rôle in a novel about India. Even more significant in the novel is the author's concern with the ultimate why, the eternal mystery of man's nature, existence, and destiny. The spiritual power revered by the novelist is the pervasive force, overshadowing the gods of the characters.

Nature, human beings, and spiritual powers are the constituents of the imagined worlds, as they are of our actual worlds. These are three dimensions of a world, not parts existing separately. The bodies of human beings are an inseparable part of the natural world; spiritual powers may be only manifestations of human ingenuity. United as they are in actuality, they must be thoroughly articulated in a novel if we as readers are to have the illusion of reality. The fusion of the three dimensions so that we have a simultaneous vision of breadth, depth, and height evokes the sense of reality which would be destroyed if we were conscious of nature as backdrop, characters as actors, and the supernatural intervening like a *deus ex machina*. Each dimension may be viewed separately only if we remember that such a view is an abstraction. It is the novelist's articulation of the three dimensions that is the ultimate source of our experience of reality, not any one dimension as a separate entity.

THE AUTHORITY OF THE NOVELIST

The articulation by the novelist constitutes a fourth dimension. This fourth dimension is real as a matter of fact. A novelist has created a world with words. The dimension is also real because it is interesting, moving, and convincing. Here, in the subtle interplay of creator and creation, lies the meaning of the novel. This is the joy of the critic and his despair. This is the source of his pleasure and insight, but the frustration of his attempt to explain it. The author is the god of his creation; he is not only alpha and omega but also jot and tittle. He is most present where least observed.

The authority of the novelist is felt rather than perceived. I feel confident when I start some novels that the novelist is securely in charge. I read with ease, not worrying in fear that the novelist will falter or fumble and betray me. The source of this confidence is to be sought not in any one element of the novel; it is rather my response to the novelist's own conviction that his characters are real. The passage has already been quoted in which James says that a novelist who admits he is only making believe is betraying his sacred office and committing "a terrible crime".[1] "In simpler words, a novelist while he writes his novel must care more about his imaginary world than about any other possible world," writes Ortega y Gasset.[2] Mr Forster has said:

> And now we can get a definition as to when a character in a book is real: it is real when the novelist knows everything about it. He may not choose to tell us all he knows — many of the facts, even of the kind we call obvious, may be hidden. But he will give us the feeling that though the

[1] "The Art of Fiction", p. 6.   [2] *Notes on the Novel*, p. 95.

character has not been explained, it is explicable, and we get from this reality of a kind we can never get in daily life.[1]

My confidence is also based on the novelist's tone. His attitude towards the characters and action must be emotionally and intellectually right if I am to lose myself in his world. When a novelist sneers at what I consider true or praises extravagantly what I consider ordinary, the disparity between what is being written and the manner of the writing forces me to be aware of the writer. Only when the tone is just right do I forget that I am reading and enter imaginatively into the world of the novel. When a character is "upset" at hearing that her only son has been kidnapped, the inadequacy of the language destroys the illusion. On the other hand, lush writing about the trivial shakes my confidence in the novelist's knowledge of people and their behaviour. The attitude of the novelist towards the imagined world he is creating must be an understanding one if I am to have confidence that he is imagining a real world at all.

Less intangible than these impressions is the security fostered by the novelist's rôle. As we have seen, the novelist must assume a rôle, since his true function as creator is destructive of credibility. What rôle best fosters illusion changes with shifts of taste and convention. In the eighteenth century the fashionable rôle was that of editor – Richardson and Defoe, for example. George Eliot is a philosopher in *Middlemarch* who comments on the action and characters both in the text and at the headings of chapters. Henry James is an historian in *The Portrait of a Lady*. In our day the fashion is for the novelist to pretend to be invisible, but some novelists refuse this rôle and like Forster in *A Passage to India* address the reader. No one rôle is more or less convincing to me. I can adjust to any rôle so long as the novelist establishes it clearly at the beginning and maintains it consistently.

The rôle of the novelist and the point of view from which the reader sees the world of the novel are related but not identical.

[1] *Aspects of the Novel*, p. 6.

Two novelists may choose to be invisible and omniscient, but in one novel the point of view may be limited to one character, while in the other it may shift among varied characters. In one the view of the main action may be close in space and time, while in the other it may be a distant view of someone remote in time and loosely connected to the action. Since what we as readers see is determined by the point from which we look, the point of view is one of the most important ways our attention is focused.

Related to both the rôle of the novelist and the point of view is the person by whom the novel is narrated. Both the first and third persons are common at all periods in the history of the novel. Moll Flanders, Pip in *Great Expectations*, and Frederic Henry in *A Farewell to Arms* tell their own stories. The narratives of *Tom Jones*, *Middlemarch*, and *The Hamlet* are in the third person.

As with the rôle of the novelist, no one point of view or person determines the reality of a novel. I can adjust to Pip's autobiography in *Great Expectations*, to Stephen's point of view in *A Portrait of the Artist as a Young Man*, to the shifting from one character to another in *The Hamlet*. What I do need if I am to lose myself in the world of the novel is that the point of view and the person be clear, controlled, and purposeful. When the point of view is used as a device to gain effects, I become conscious of the device and I resent being manipulated. The more complexly the point of view and the person function in revealing the meaning of the novelist the less aware I am of them as devices and the more aware I am of the reality of the imagined world. For example, the point of view of Marlow and his narrative in the first person are conspicuous in *Lord Jim*, but they are convincing because he functions in terms of place, time, action, human behaviour, and metaphysical implications. That some readers identify Marlow with Conrad is proof of the artistry with which Conrad has created the character. He seems so real he is spoken of as actual. My belief in his credibility creates belief in the world he inhabits. It is not the inordinate length of his after-dinner story which destroys the illusion of reality, but the premature ending and shift to an unnamed man in London.

THE DENSE WEB

Like the authority of the novelist, the dense web catches our attention at first and then we quickly lose consciousness of it in our absorption in the action. This phrase, "a dense web", is quoted from Ortega y Gasset. In order that the imagined world may seem real, he said, "the reader must be caught in a dense web of innumerable minutely told circumstances. What is our life but an immense agglomeration of trifles?"[1] James also emphasizes "truth of detail".

> One can speak best from one's own taste, and I may therefore venture to say that the air of reality (solidity of specification) seems to me to be the supreme virtue of a novel – the merit on which all its other merits (including that conscious moral purpose of which Mr Besant speaks) helplessly and submissively depend.[2]

The solidity of specification is all the more important because we as readers are usually as unconscious of it as we are of the ground under our feet.

Since the agglomeration of trifles in our lives is immense, a novelist must suggest this agglomeration with the creation of a few. Those few strengthen the illusion not through their correspondence to actuality (any detail would correspond to the actual because all details might) but through relation to the whole vision the novelist is communicating. That is why James can speak of this solidity of specification as "the supreme virtue of a novel". In his own *The Portrait of a Lady* he is writing about a young woman who wishes "to see". Throughout the novel we are constantly aware of the eyes of the characters.[3] Henrietta Stackpole has "a peculiarly open, surprised-looking eye".[4] The eyes of the Misses Molyneux

---

[1] *Notes on the Novel*, p. 97.   [2] "The Art of Fiction", p. 14.

[3] Dorothy Van Ghent in *The English Novel, Form and Function*, has an illuminating essay on this subject.   [4] Boston, 1881, I, 116.

were "like the balanced basins, the circles of 'ornamental water', set, in parterres, among the geraniums", and "round, quiet, and contented".[1] Of Gilbert Osmond we read, "His conscious, curious eyes, however, eyes at once vague and penetrating, intelligent and hard, expressive of the observer as well as of the dreamer, would have assured you that he studied it only within well-chosen limits, and that in so far as he sought it he found it." [2] These many references to eyes are only one part of a texture which includes references to doors and windows, to lights and shade, to paintings, statues, china, and coins. In *Lord Jim* we are often in darkness with flickering or soft lights: moon, stars, candle, lamp, lantern, bonfire, cigar tips. The texture of *The Hamlet* has the ugly threads of "the barren yard littered with the rubbish – the ashes, the shards of pottery and tin cans – of its last tenants" [3] and the beautiful threads of dusk, "the shortening twilight of late April, in which the blanched dogwoods stood among the darker trees with spread raised palms like praying nuns; there was the evening star and already the whippoorwills".[4]

The world of *The Hamlet* is also full of animals: horses, ponies, mules, cows, and dogs are prominent throughout. The animals are there not just as natural elements of the country nor even to reveal human character, although they do both. They are also part of the figurative design. The similes and metaphors are concrete details also. They form a secondary design which enriches the texture. For example, in *The Hamlet* one of the Snopes is called Mink; another has "bright quick, amoral eyes like a chipmunk"; a third has a "rodent's face"; the two daughters of Ab Snopes are like heifers.[5] Ratliff says, "Only this here seems to be a different kind of Snopes like a cotton-mouth is a different kind of snake." [6] Later Faulkner writes about Ratliff:

> What he felt was outrage at the waste, the useless
> squandering; at a situation intrinsically and inherently

---

[1] Boston, 1881, I, 104.   [2] Ibid., I, 328.
[3] Modern Library, New York, 1931, p. 20.
[4] Ibid., p. 24.   [5] Ibid., pp. 162, 163.   [6] Ibid., p. 92.

wrong by any economy, like building a log dead-fall and baiting it with a freshened heifer to catch a rat; or no, worse: as though the gods themselves had funneled all the concentrated bright wet-slanted unparadised June onto a dung-heap, breeding pismires.[1]

Most repulsive of all the Snopes is Flem. Flem is "froglike", with eyes "the colour of stagnant water", a face "as blank as a pan of uncooked dough", with "a tiny predatory nose like the beak of a small hawk", "with a good deal of the quality of a spider of that bulbous blond omnivorous though non-poisonous species".[2]

In novel after novel the details of the physical world and the figures of speech are woven together into a meaningful and effective design. In *The Portrait of a Lady* Gilbert Osmond's house is described as having "the mask, not the face of the house. It had heavy lids, but no eyes; the house in reality looked another way – looked off behind, into splendid openness and the range of the afternoon light."[3] Conrad describes Patusan as follows:

> Again, in the exposed part of the town big fires blazed along the only street, revealing from distance to distance upon their glares the falling straight lines of roofs, the fragments of wattled walls jumbled in confusion, here and there a whole hut elevated in the glow upon the vertical black stripes of a group of high piles; and all this line of dwellings, revealed in patches by the swaying flames, seemed to flicker tortuously away upriver into the gloom at the heart of the land.[4]

Middlemarch is full of vistas, both as part of the scene and as figures of speech.[5]

[1] *The Hamlet*, pp. 162–3.   [2] Ibid., pp. 22–3, 52, 59.
[3] I, 325.

[4] *Lord Jim*, Modern Library, New York, 1931, p. 373.

[5] For a thorough exposition of this subject see Mark Schorer, "Fiction and the 'Analogical Matrix' ", *Critiques and Essays on Modern Fiction*, Aldridge, New York, 1952, pp. 83–98.

For me one of the greatest rewards of re-reading a good novel is the discovery of its texture. The patterns of detail and imagery reveal new meanings and subtleties of implication. In the dense web I find one very important source for the complex experience I have had and find increased pleasure in awareness of meaning and artistry.

THE PEOPLE

Sense impressions, facts, and imagery contribute to make the characters come alive as people. The passages quoted above evoke mental images of people so that we picture them in our mind's eye as flesh and blood. Sometimes the salient physical characteristic is strongly marked and repeated as a stimulant to our imaginations. The blond hair of Jim in *Lord Jim*, the post-office mouth of Wemmick in *Great Expectations*, the spitting of Flem Snopes are only three familiar examples of physical details which emphasize character through image.

My mental image evokes feeling. Sometimes the feeling is simple repulsion, as it is for Flem Snopes. Sometimes the feeling is more complicated, as it is for Gilbert Osmond, whose appearance is attractive and yet sinister. The stronger or the more complicated my feelings for a character, the more real he becomes. Mental image is only one source of my feelings. Everything the character says and does and thinks affects my response to him. Everything other characters say and do and think about him affects my response. As I penetrate farther and farther into the imagined world, my feelings change. Sometimes they may be reversed: a simple dislike turns to liking. Other times they are intensified; a repulsive character becomes exceedingly repulsive. More often the changes are subtle: an arrogant person is courageous in adversity, which is admirable though the arrogance is annoying. Moreover, I feel slightly differently towards each character. The characters do not seem to me real if my feeling for one is just like my feeling for another. I dislike all the Snopes family, and for good reasons, but my dislike for Mink is very different from my dislike for Ab or for Io and all of them for Flem.

Some element of pity, contempt, amusement, or respect is involved in my dislike for the others, but Flem is too hard to be pitied, too clever to be contemptuous of, too cruel to be amused at, too evil to be respected.

The result of awareness of my strong, mixed, changing, and individual feelings is awareness of a pattern of feelings. It is the pattern of my feelings, evoked by the design of the book, which is one source of a novel's power. Let us take *Emma*, for example. On the fringes of the world are people for whom I feel practically nothing: Mr Cox, Mr Perry, Mrs Goddard, the Coles, Mrs Ford. Next is a group for whom my feeling is clear and simple but not strong: the Martins, the Westons, Isabella and John Knightley, Mrs Bates. Thirdly, there are the bores – Mr Woodhouse, Miss Bates, and Mrs Elton – but each is boring in such a distinctive way that the quality of my sympathy and amusement is markedly different. Finally come the principals. Mr Knightley I learn to appreciate more and more; Mr Elton I increasingly detest; for Frank Churchill my feelings are mixed since I find myself attracted by his charm while disturbed by his selfishness. The trio of women is equally diversified. I like Jane Fairfax but find her behaviour puzzling; I feel sorry for Harriet Smith at the same time that I am amused by her shallowness; for Emma my feelings are both mixed and changing. I admire her patience with her father while distressed by her blindness towards Mr Elton and Harriet and annoyed by her snobbishness and desire to be a little god. My respect for her rises with her self-control, insight, and regret.

Such a sketch of my feelings is, of course, no more than a sketch. The purpose of including it is to illustrate that the imagined world becomes real through the diversified pattern of feelings. If I felt just as strongly about Robert Martin as I do about the other men characters in *Emma*, the imagined world would lose perspective and depth. All the characters would exist on the same plane and the sense of reality would be lost. In the actual world we experience this same range of feeling. Each one of us has a circumference of people who are no more than names, a circle of acquaintances, a special group of *bêtes noires*, and an inner circle of relatives and friends.

Just as each one of us has a wide range of feelings, so each one of us has a private inner world in constant interaction with the outer world. We objectify our hostility and love; we project our images of ourselves and of other people; we try to realize our fantasies. At the same time other people and nature are resisting or co-operating with us; and our feelings, imaginations, and fantasies are altering under the pressure of outside circumstances. One of the troublesome facts of life is that my inside is always in contact with other people's outside. I am always inside myself but outside of others. I can catch fleeting glimpses of the insides of others as they can of mine, but the glimpse is always fleeting. The revelation is usually startling. The inside is so often unpredictable and at odds with the outside.

The world of many a novel turns on this point of interaction between an inner and outer world. I think at once of Pip's expectations, of Jim's dreams of glory, of Isabel's desire to see, of Stephen's changing fantasies, and of Dorothea's need to serve others. The characters become alive for me because their inner lives are constantly affecting and being affected by the outer world as mine is.

Moreover, the complexity of the inner life is channelled by our bodies into a single line of action. We may be capable of more than one profession or of more than one marriage. Many lines of action may appeal to us for varied and even contradictory reasons. Many possible speeches may be dictated by our feelings. Nevertheless, we can do only one thing at a time and say only one thing at a time. Miss Elizabeth Bowen has expressed this as follows:

Action is the simplification (for story purposes) of complexity. For each one act, there are an x number of rejected alternatives. It is the palpable presence of the alternatives that gives action interest. Therefore, in each of the characters, while he or she is acting, the play and pull of alternatives must be felt. It is in being seen to be capable of alternatives that the character becomes, for the reader, valid.[1]

As each alternative is chosen, consequences of action follow. The consequences are not necessarily mainly for others. The emotional repercussions of one's own words and actions may be more significant than anything others may say or do in consequence. Characters vary in their sensitivities just as people do. Some are capable of major changes in attitudes; others remain the same no matter what is said or done to them. Characters become real to me when the rate and nature of their change or their lack of change varies.

In summary, characters become real to me when I have a physical image of them; when I feel strong, mixed, changing, and particular feelings for them; when I see the interaction of their inner and outer lives; when I observe their choices among alternatives; and when I am convinced that their change or lack of change is a natural consequence of their choices. These five sources of reality need to be stressed because the most common reason given for finding a character real is not to my mind a valid one. This reason is that the character is human if he has vices and weaknesses. This reason finds its equivalent in actuality when people say of another, "After all, he's only human," meaning that the person has demonstrated some fault or folly. The unconscious assumption is, of course, that the basic nature of humanity is evil and weak. Another unconscious assumption is that a human being is composed of qualities, separable entities, each of which may be neatly labelled and classified as "Good" or "Evil". Each person is assumed to contain varying numbers of these entities. If a character has only good qualities or only bad qualities, he then is called "unreal". According to this theory a real character has a mixture of "good" and "bad". To my mind both assumptions are wrong. I think our virtues make us human, and I think we have characteristics neither good nor

[1] "Notes on Writing a Novel", *Collected Impressions*, New York, 1950, p. 251.

bad in themselves which result in some circumstances in good and in others in evil.

That character is plot is a truism of literary criticism. Like many another truism, the statement is true only in the most obvious and least significant sense. Certainly we lose any illusion of actuality if characters are made to perform actions which seem uncharacteristic, especially if we see that the novelist is more concerned with surprising us than with depicting natural human behaviour. The characters must appear to determine the plot, if we are to lose ourselves successfully in the reality of the imagined world. However, human beings are more complex than their actions are, and consequently characters and plot cannot be related in any simple equation.

The plot of a novel is not merely the sum of the actions of the characters. The plot is the events as they are related to each other. The action of the novel must start. What starts it? The action has consequences. What determines the consequences? The action ends. What brings it to an end? As Mr Forster has said, "A plot is also a narrative of events, the emphasis falling on causality."[1] The characters may seem to determine the plot; but the novelist creates it. "Why did this happen to me?" is the common cry of bewildered humanity. The answer in a novel to the mystery of human existence is found in the plot.

The answer may be human nature. Such an answer merely raises new questions. What kinds of actions bring what kinds of results? In *Great Expectations* Pip gives a pie to Magwitch. That one act is both good and bad. Pip is blessed for feeding the hungry and guilty of stealing, lying, and aiding an escaped convict. The complex nature of the act has complex results. Before Pip was born, his destiny was being formed. The evil deeds of Compeyson have led to the corruption of Magwitch

---

[1] *Aspects of the Novel*, p. 82. Cf. Van Ghent, *The English Novel, Form and Function*, p. 6: "The novel is able to express the most profound ideas, but, because of the nature of this medium, these will lie implicitly in the conjunction of events that are bodied forth. The ideas in a novel are largely for the reader's inference, his inference of the principles by which the happenings in the book are related to each other."

and Arthur Havisham and the derangement of Miss Havisham.
Pip and Estelle are the innocent victims of the spreading evil.
The evil is not triumphant. Redemption comes through insight and forgiveness. No villain initiates the action in *A
Passage to India*, only good intentions. Adele Quested is eager
to see India; Mrs Moore is filled with Christian love; Dr Aziz
is courteous; Fielding is friendly to people of all races; Professor Godbole is devoutly religious. And yet the seemingly
harmless picnic to the Marabar Caves is a fiasco. The action
turns again. The finale is not disastrous. Mrs Moore dies, but
her spirit lives on. Adele comes to her senses just in time to
save Dr Aziz and herself. Dr Aziz is professionally ruined, but
he does not sue Adele for exorbitant damages. At the end it is
the sky and not a character which prevents Aziz and Fielding
from being friends. To say that character is plot is not enough.
What we seek to discover is what characteristics result in what
kinds of actions, reactions, and final consequences.

Character is also suspect because it is an old word. The
word suggests that an individual's will is the ultimate power.
The implication is that everyone can control his actions and is
thus responsible for his condition. Virtue, health, and success
come to those who want them and make the requisite effort.
Anyone who is sick, poor, or wicked is deservedly so. Although
this view is still popularly held, studies of biologists, sociolog-
ists, and psychologists have rendered obsolete this explanation
of the human condition. Today a scientifically inclined novelist
may consider that heredity is plot or that environment is plot
or that the subconscious is plot.

The opinion that the characters in any sense determine the
plot may be rejected by a novelist in favour of natural or
supernatural powers which override our wills, intentions, and
desires and control our destinies, however much we may seem
to be acting freely.

The plot of a novel is thus more than the revelation of character through their actions. The plot is the soul of the novel.
Through the relations of events, through the causes of complication and of *dénouement*, the novelist communicates his

insight into the meaning of life and his belief in the powers that be.

THE POWERS THAT BE

The novelist's vision of the ultimate and binding force in the world and the religious beliefs of the characters are not necessarily the same. That the characters do have religious beliefs is one source of their verisimilitude, and that they should in varying degrees live in accordance with their beliefs is also part of the verisimilitude. It is true, too, of human beings in life as it is of characters in novels that their ostensible religious affiliation may be only nominal and that at heart they are worshipping a very different god.

Emma is a good example of a novel in which author and character seem to be at one in paying lip service to religion but in having a profound belief in human judgement. God plays no part in the lives of the characters, although Mr Elton is a clergyman and Emma goes to church unless the weather is too cold. It is the social status of Mr Elton's profession which is important, not his Christian vocation. The real power in the novel is the power of common sense. When Emma is fearfully contemplating a marriage between Mr Knightley and Harriet, she asks herself, "Was it new for anything in this world to be unequal, inconsistent, incongruous – or for chance and circumstance (as second causes) to direct the human fate?"[1] But, when Mr Knightley does propose to her and she sees that Harriet has been deluded, the world is revealed as equal, consistent, congruous, with human judgement deciding human fate.

> She felt for Harriet, with pain and with contrition; but no flight of generosity run mad, opposing all that could be probable or reasonable, entered her brain. She had led her friend astray, and it would be a reproach to her for ever; but her judgment was as strong as her feelings, and as strong as it had ever been before, in reprobating any such alliance for him, as most unequal and degrading.[2]

[1] Jane Austen, *Emma*, Oxford, The World's Classics, 1946, p. 368.
[2] Ibid., p. 383.

A major theme of both English and American novels is the inadequacy of Christianity and the displacement of the Christian God by more potent forces. *A Passage to India* has already been cited as a novel in which the characters have many different religious beliefs. Mr Forster himself believes in the holiness of the heart's affections. Christianity, Hinduism, and Mohammedanism are separated by chasms too deep for the intellect to bridge, but Mrs Moore, Professor Godbole, and Dr Aziz are united by a mystical love beyond their own understanding. In *Lord Jim* the safe and limited Christianity of Jim's father, the English vicar, is contrasted with the inscrutable malice of the Dark Powers. Conrad's own belief is in the mysterious incomprehensibility of life. When Jim met his death, did he behold "the face of that opportunity which, like an Eastern bride, had come veiled to his side", or did he go away "from a living woman to celebrate his pitiless wedding with a shadowy ideal of conduct"?[1] Was Jim a real person or a "disembodied spirit"? Neither Marlow who raises these questions nor Conrad answers them decisively.

A return to myth as the ultimate truth has been a distinctive feature of twentieth-century novels. Two conspicuous examples of the belief of novelists in the power of Greek myth are *A Portrait of the Artist as a Young Man* and *The Hamlet*. There is no mistaking the fact that Joyce intends us to think of Greek myth in *A Portrait*. We are not reading symbolism into the novel. From the quotation from Ovid on the title page to the final words about "old artificer" we are reminded constantly of Dedalus and his son Icarus. What is not clear to me is whether Stephen's vision is a true vision of reality or a fantasy. Is the implication of Stephen's last words, "Old Father, old artificer, stand me now and ever in good stead", that he like Icarus will fly too high and be punished by his *hybris*?[2] This novel is perennially fascinating to me because Joyce poses the question, "What is real?" without providing a decisive answer. The calls of many religions ring through the novel: the calls of athleticism, of worldly success, of Irish nationalism,

[1] P. 416.   [2] P. 253.

of Roman Catholicism. Is the call of the "fabulous artificer" "a symbol of the artist forging anew in his workshop out of the sluggish matter of the earth, a new soaring impalpable imperishable being"?[1] Is it truly "the call of life to his soul"?[2] Is he "a priest of eternal imagination, transmuting the daily bread of experience into the radiant body of everliving life"[3] or is he a Lucifer doomed to fall through eternity because he says in his pride, "I will not serve"?[4]

No such ambiguity obscures the meaning of *The Hamlet*. Mr Faulkner makes unmistakably clear that Greek myth is being re-enacted in Mississippi. Eula's "entire appearance suggested some symbology out of the old Dionysic times . . ."[5] He writes of a "Pan-hallowed retreat" and of "Olympian legs" and of Troy's Helen and Juno. The result is interesting, but to me not convincing. The incongruity between the cow and Juno and between the fat cold potato-eating Eula and the Olympian gods is too strong for me to make the kind of connection that I think Mr Faulkner expects the reader to make.

In other novels the myth is less obvious. Here the difficulty begins. Starting with the recognition that in some novels myth is the essential power, some critics have then looked for myth in every novel. The experiences of birth and re-birth, trial and initiation, the death of the old and the growth of the new are so basic to human life that it is no wonder the critics looking for the myth of the Old Year and the New Year can find it in almost any novel. In the United States, in particular, civilization has so recently been superimposed upon the primitive that the mythic implications of the hunt and man's abode in the forest and cave are plain in both life and in literature. The myths that naturally evolve from the rhythms of light and dark, of the four seasons, and of the ages of man are potent indeed when released subtly in a novel and when responded to subtly. We reduce the meaning and limit the power of novels like Conrad's *Heart of Darkness* and Virginia Woolf's *To the Lighthouse* when we try to equate image with symbol. The lighthouse means more than any definition. For some novelists

[1] P. 169.   [2] Ibid.   [3] P. 221.   [4] P. 239   [5] P. 95.

the powers that be are all the inscrutable impulses accumu-
lated through centuries by man and heaped without order in
the dusky caves of our collective subconscious. For others the
sky is stronger than the cave.

ARTICULATION

The novelist creates a three-dimensional world. The significance of the world lies not only in the nature of each dimension but also in the proportions of each dimension.[1] In *Emma*,
for example, the human dimension is paramount. Trees are
important only as signs of wealth and social position; religion is
only a social convention. Contrast with this a novel by Hardy
or Lawrence where both the physical and spiritual rival the
human in interest and significance. The novelist's vision of
reality is communicated through his proportion and emphasis;
his skill is observable only when not observed. When we become conscious of a tree as unrelated to the human beings and
their values or to the existence of a spiritual force, then the
tree becomes unreal. In other words, in a novel the illusion of
reality is achieved through sensitive relationships perceived
and communicated by the novelist.

The art required to achieve this illusion is all the more to
be admired when we recognize that the three dimensions are
communicated to us through one. The novel is linear. It has
a beginning, middle, and end. No matter how simultaneously
the three dimensions would interact in actuality, in the novel
one detail must precede or follow another. The relationship between the whole imagined world on the one hand and the order
in the novel on the other comprises the structure. Because of
the basic importance of the story line, some critics think the element of time the most important of all the elements in a novel.

[1] Virginia Woolf comments on a novelist's perspective: "All alone we
must climb upon the novelist's shoulders and gaze through his eyes until
we, too, understand in what order he ranges the large common objects
upon which novelists are fated to gaze: man and men; behind them
Nature; and above them that power which for convenience and brevity
we may call God." "Robinson Crusoe", *The Second Common Reader*,
New York, 1932, pp. 51–2.

How much time is involved in the action? How much of the past affects the present? Is the past implied, casually referred to, extensively depicted in flashbacks? Is the present fully explored in a series of scenes or summarized in narrative? How much of the future is implied or stated at the end? How clearly is the future foreseen and anticipated in the course of the action? These are all significant questions of structure.[1]

The reader's knowledge is also involved in the structure of the novel. At every point we as readers know either more or less than the characters about what has happened, what is happening, and what will happen. We come as strangers into a world where characters know themselves and others. Some novelists mystify us by presenting the action in such an order that the characters know more than we do. In *Lord Jim*, for instance, we are at Jim's trial before we know that the *Patna* did not sink, although all the characters know this. Other novelists will narrate in detail important action so that our interest as readers is directed towards the reactions of the characters as they discover and interpret this action. George Eliot's handling of the death of Raffles in *Middlemarch* is an example.

Preparation and surprise are not simply narrative devices, but part of the meaning of the novel. Meaningful also is the end of the novel. The double meaning of *end* emphasizes its importance. An end is both a conclusion and a goal. The end is both the culmination of the action, the point towards which all action has led, and the finale. The integrity of the end is extremely important. A contrived happy ending shocks us with its artifice. An inept ending with many loose threads is not satisfying. An abrupt and peremptory ending destroys any illusion of reality. An ending, to be real, must follow naturally from previous action, must imply a future for the characters, and must enforce the central point of the novel.

Articulation means both the joining of parts and utterance.

[1] Two good books on this subject are Phyllis Bentley, *Some Observations on the Art of Narrative*, New York, 1947, and Edwin Muir, *The Structure of the Novel*, London, 1928.

When we come to the consideration of language, we have come to the end of our search for what in a novel evokes our sense of reality. A novel is composed of words in sentences. The novelist's style is ultimately the source of our experience. "We have come full circle." When we start a novel, we respond at once to the style. When we finish the novel, the style lingers with us. At every point between, style operates on us, however low our awareness may be. The novelist, as I have already said, is alpha and omega, jot and tittle.

In most novels the uniformity of the style acts as a subtle, unifying, and reassuring force. Once we have accepted as authoritative the style of the author, its recurrent and familiar pattern helps to convince us of the reality of the vision. *Emma*, *Middlemarch*, and *The Portrait of a Lady* are good examples of novels written in distinctive styles.

> Human nature is so well disposed towards those who are in interesting situations, that a young person, who either marries or dies, is sure of being kindly spoken of.[1]

> I suppose it was that in courtship everything is regarded as provisional and preliminary, and the smallest sample of virtue or accomplishment is taken to guarantee delightful stores which the broad leisure of marriage will reveal. But the doorsill of marriage once crossed, expectation is concentrated on the present. Having once embarked on your marital voyage, it is impossible not to be aware that you make no way, and that the sea is not within sight – that, in fact, you are exploring an inclosed basin.[2]

> She had felt at the same time that he was helpless and ineffectual, but the feeling had taken the form of a tenderness which was the very flower of respect. He was like a sceptical voyager strolling on the beach while he waited for the tide, looking seaward yet not putting to sea. It was in all this she had found her occasion. She would launch his

[1] *Emma*, p. 157.

[2] *Middlemarch*, ed. Gordon S. Haight, Boston, Riverside edition, 1956, p. 145.

boat for him; she would be his providence; it would be a good thing to love him.[1]

These three comments on marriage need no footnotes for the alert reader. The style of each is typical of the world the novelist has created.

In our century novelists have developed in various ways the art of changing styles in a novel. Joyce, in *A Portrait of the Artist as a Young Man*, reveals the growth of the child to the man through the changing language appropriate to his age. The following quotations are illustrations of an artist's growth.

> His father told him that story: his father looked at him through a glass: he had a hairy face.
> He was baby tuckoo.[2]

> Only God could do that. He tried to think what a big thought that must be but he could think only of God. God was God's name just as his name was Stephen. *Dieu* was the French for God and that was God's name too; and when anyone prayed to God and said *Dieu* then God knew at once that it was a French person that was praying.[3]

> – Stephanos Dedalos! Bous Stephanoumenes! Bous Stephaneforos!
> Their banter was not new to him and now it flattered his mild proud sovereignty. Now, as never before, his strange name seemed to him a prophecy. So timeless seemed the grey warm air, so fluid and impersonal his own mood, that all ages were as one to him. A moment before the ghost of the ancient kingdom of the Danes had looked forth through the vesture of the hazewrapped city. Now, at the name of the fabulous artificer, he seemed to hear the noise of dim waves and to see a winged form flying above the waves and slowly climbing the air.[4]

As an incipient artist Stephen is naturally interested in words. As a boy he puzzles about the various meanings of *belt* and the

---

[1] *The Portrait of a Lady*, II, 172.
[2] *A Portrait of the Artist as a Young Man*, p. 7.
[3] Ibid., p. 16. [4] Ibid., p. 168.

ugliness of *suck*. After leaving Clongowes, Stephen studies words. "Words which he did not understand he said over and over to himself till he had learnt them by heart: and through them he had glimpses of the real world about him."[1] At the moment of ecstasy when he hears the call to be an artist, he thinks of words.

> He drew forth a phrase from his treasure and spoke it softly to himself:
>
> – A day of dappled seaborne clouds. –
>
> The phrase and the day and the scene harmonized in a chord. Words. Was it their colours? He allowed them to glow and fade, hue after hue: sunrise gold, the russet and green of apple orchards, azure of waves, the greyfringed fleece of clouds. No, it was not their colours: it was the poise and balance of the period itself. Did he then love the rhythmic rise and fall of words better than their associations of legend and colour? Or was it that, being as weak of sight as he was shy of mind, he drew less pleasure from the reflection of the glowing sensible world through the prism of a language many coloured and richly storied than from the contemplation of an inner world of individual emotions mirrored perfectly in a lucid supple periodic prose?[2]

Among American novelists William Faulkner is distinctive for versatility of style as well as for the uniqueness of the one style usually associated with him. Within one page we find the two sentences:

> It holds in tranquil paradox of suspended precipitation dawn, noon, and sunset; yesterday, today, and tomorrow – star spawn and hieroglyph, the fierce white dying rose, then gradual and invincible speeding up to and into slack-flood's coronal of nympholept noon.

> It was after sunset when Houston returned home and missed the cow.[3]

---

[1] *A Portrait of the Artist as a Young Man*, p. 62.
[2] Ibid., p. 166. [3] *The Hamlet*, pp. 188–9.

Through diction and sentence structure Mr Faulkner is affecting our attitude towards Ike and Houston. Houston is the kind of person to whom a sunset is a sunset and a cow is a cow. Ike the idiot, Mr Faulkner would have us believe, looks with wonder at a strange and beautiful world in which a well is for him "a still and insatiable aperture of earth" and a cow a Juno and a Helen of Troy. By responding to the diction, we may respond to the significance of scene or action which Faulkner sees in it.

When Joyce and Faulkner and other modern novelists withdraw from the kind of active participation in a narrative that nineteenth-century novelists like James, Conrad, and George Eliot engaged in, they re-entered the novel even more obviously through their style. The conspicuousness of the style may be one reason for the recent trend in the criticism of the novel to emphasize language. That language is of the utmost importance I would agree. What, after all, is a novel if not words in sentences? Language is not a separate element in the art of the novelist; it *is* the art. No novel can be good unless it is well written. As Mr Daiches says, "The phrase 'writes well' seems to distinguish between what is written and what is written *about*, and this is a false distinction in imaginative literature." [1]

We have been searching in the novel for the source of our experience of reality, and we have found it to be technique. This may seem at first glance a disappointment. Technique carries associations of engineering, of craft and skill, rather than of artistry. Clearly, the word *technique* is in literary criticism used with meanings not elsewhere common. Mr Mark Schorer's article, "Technique as Discovery", is the best exposition I know of the meaning of technique.

For technique is the means by which the writer's experience, which is his subject matter, compels him to attend to it; technique is the only means he has of discovering, exploring,

[1] David Daiches, "The Nature of Fiction", *A Study of Literature for Readers and Critics*, Ithaca, New York, 1948, p. 57.

developing his subject, of conveying its meaning, and finally, of evaluating it.

Technique in fiction is, of course, all those obvious forms of it which are usually taken to be the whole of it, and many others; but for the present purposes, let it be thought of in two respects particularly: the uses to which language, as language, is put to express the quality of the experience in question; and the uses of point of view not only as a mode of dramatic delimitation, but more particularly, of thematic definition. Technique is really what T. S. Eliot means by "convention" – any selection, structure, or distortion, any form or rhythm imposed upon the world of action; by means of which – it should be added – our apprehension of the world of action is enriched or renewed. In this sense, everything is technique which is not the lump of experience itself.[1]

At this point you may well raise an objection. "If, as you say, technique (which includes style) is the ultimate source of our sense of reality, why don't you as a critic begin with a consideration of the style of a novel? Why should you begin with your experience or even bother to speak of imagined worlds?" The answer is that some critics do begin with style. The end is always a logical beginning, and style in being the material of a novel is one end. The difficulty I find in beginning with style is the nature of language which fulfils its function best when unnoticed. The function of language in a novel, as we saw in the first chapter, is to create an image in the reader's mind of a real world. The end of a novel is then the image in the reader's mind. The critic, beginning with this end, discovers its source in technique.[2]

VISION

"Technique is vision."[3] In this one sentence we have the guide for our next step. If technique were a skill, our next step

---

[1] *Critiques and Essays on Modern Fiction*, pp. 67, 68.

[2] Cf. Philip Rahv, "Fiction and the Criticism of Fiction", *The Kenyon Review*, XVIII (Spring 1956) 276–99.

[3] Van Ghent, p. 127.

would be to study how the illusion was created. We would approach the novel as if it were a jigsaw puzzle, the parts cleverly cut asunder by a master's saw and awaiting our cleverness in discerning the cuts and re-assembling them. But, if technique is vision, we are directed to look at what the novelist's vision means for us.

The vision of the novelist means first of all, "This world is real." Such a statement is no light one to make. Amid the flux and chaos of the actual world each one of us has a desperate struggle all his life to arrive at the point where we can say that simple statement with assurance. We are constantly in doubt about the reality of our images of people and places, of the kinds of consequences of actions, of our religious beliefs. We encounter very different worlds, each of which seems real. How can we reconcile them? A novelist, by his assurance that this world of his is real, gives us a moment's surcease from our restless seeking and uncertainty.

Moreover, when a novelist says, "this world is real", he says it with expression. The tone of his voice reveals his attitude towards his vision. He deplores it or wonders at it or shrugs it off or denounces it or glorifies it. The vision of a novel includes both what is seen and the attitude towards what is seen. Sometimes the attitude is the more noteworthy of the two. Others assert the reality of violence, but who else has asserted it with the complexity of attitude evinced by Mr Faulkner? The attitude of the novelist towards his vision constitutes the morality of the novel.

That the novelist's vision and his attitude towards it constitute his meaning and morality is a crucial point in understanding the art of the novel. Certain popular misconceptions need to be firmly dealt with because they wreak such havoc. One of these is that meaning is a message. A novelist is not a preacher trying to convert his readers with an appeal to a gospel; he is not a teacher trying to make a lesson clear. A novelist's meaning cannot be re-stated in exposition. He does not put things in a nutshell or "sell" anything with a slogan. His meaning is infinitely more varied than the sum of the words on the page because his meaning includes our responses. Another common misconception is that meaning must be generalization. According to this view, Mr Faulkner must mean that every town is like Frenchman's Bend or Jane Austen must mean that every town is like Highbury. In fact, meaning is as particular as the world portrayed. A novelist starts with the given; a reader must accept the given. What Mr Faulkner is saying is, "Given these people in this place, these are the consequences".

The meaning of *morality* is also open to misconception. The commonest misconception is, of course, to ascribe the morals of the characters to the author. Since the novelist creates the actions of the characters, the argument goes, he is morally responsible for what they do. In reply, the counter argument is that the novelist is morally responsible only for his attitude and actions and not for those of others. The proper questions to ask are, "What is the novelist's moral standard? What is his scale of values? What is the axis? What are the poles?" That evil may triumph over good at the end of the novel does not prove the novelist immoral unless his attitude reveals that such a triumph pleases him. The morality of a novel cannot be evaded by a catch-phrase like "Art for art's sake". The creation of a world is an act which involves the creator morally. On the other hand, the morality of the creator is not to be judged by the morality of the creatures or by conventional standards of proper conduct or language.

Since meaning is implicit in the vision and morality is implicit in the tone, a reader must be very sensitive to implications to perceive them. Of all the demands made upon the reader, this is the most difficult because the most subtle. It is also the most rewarding. These are the values which endure from one reading to another, from generation to generation, and century to century.

A vision is communicated to us through the act of publication. It is presented for each of us to evaluate for himself. The source of the vision in the novelist's psyche, his life, his society may be interesting, but it is irrelevant. A novel is not a journal designed to reveal the self. No, the novel has been published for us so that we can see the vision the novelist has seen.

Our evaluation of a novel is not a judgement of its quality. That would mean a shift of metaphor and a serious distortion of the critical process. A judge is faced with defendant and prosecutor. He is superior to both. Appeal is only possible to a higher judge. We ought rather to keep the metaphor of vision. In comparison with the novelist, our vision is limited and circumscribed. We have seen little of life and recognized little of its meaning. We evaluate a novel not by comparing the novelist's vision with ours (as if our vision were the standard of excellence) but by comparing our vision with the novelist's. How much more does he see than we do? That is the crucial question. What is the depth of his vision? What is his scope? What is his acuteness? What does he feel and think about his vision? The more we see and feel that we have not seen and felt before, the better we say the novel is.

DISCRIMINATION

Our recognition of the quality of the vision leads us then to a statement of the value of the novel. We can securely discriminate between a good novel and a bad if we are aware of the intention of the novelist, of the nature of the novel, and of our experience in reading the novel and what evoked the experience. This is our goal as I set it forth in the Preface. I would end this chapter here, if the nature of our goal and its value had never been questioned. The question often asked by implication if not explicitly is, "When you say 'this novel is good', what exactly do you mean?"

First of all, I mean it is a good *novel*. A book may be a bad novel and yet a good book. We need first of all as critics to be sure that the book we have read is a novel at all. A bad novel may be a good poem, play, or short story. It may be good journalism, history, autobiography, case study, or satire. More difficult to distinguish from novels are fantasy, fable, and formula. A fantasy is good if it furnishes "release from the actualities of time and place, or an escape valve for pent-up emotions".[1] A fable may serve a very useful purpose as propaganda. It may improve social conditions by arousing emotional support for reform or it may convey ideas in a form easy to perceive and assimilate.[2] A formula may provide relaxation and entertainment for the weary and troubled. We may be caught in a crisis in which all our energy is needed to cope with actuality. Then we may want a "good" book but not a good novel. For some, such a book is a detective story, a western story, a love story, a success story, or science fiction.

Secondly, good means *good*, not perfect. Achievement is always costly. One effect is gained only through the sacrifices of others. The prefaces of Henry James are eloquent testimony to the painful choices which a novelist makes. We show our ignorance of both art and life if we expect a novelist to satisfy all our demands simultaneously no matter how contradictory they may be. Moreover, a good novel may have flaws: a jolting shift in point of view, a weak scene, a lifeless character, a colourless background. However, I have learned to be wary of denouncing "flaws" in novels. I have learned to ask myself, "What is the effect of this jolt or that weakness?" Often the effect is seen to have value. For example, Caspar Goodwood in *The Portrait of a Lady* has been condemned as a wooden character. I find him unattractive. But so did Isabel. Wasn't our feeling of his deadness part of the emotional design of the novel?

Thirdly, a good novel is *good* for us. It gives us pleasure by transporting us out of our lives, by stirring and satisfying our emotions, and by stimulating our imaginations. The aesthetic delight in consummate artistry is one of the purest pleasures and greatest goods available to us. We grow as people through the extension of our capacity for imagining and feeling for the lives of others. Vicarious experience may be as potent a force in our spiritual lives as any actual experience, more potent sometimes because more vivid and penetrating than anything our meagre lives can offer without totally shattering us in the

[1] Gerould, *How to Read Fiction*, pp. 8–12.
[2] Daiches, "The Nature of Fiction", p. 60.

process. As we grow in our understanding of what is real, we may develop an ethical code with a sturdy foundation. Ideals of what should be can produce good only if united with a clear insight into what is. Novels, by helping us to find a world we can call real, help us towards a sound system of values.

Fourthly, a good novel is good for *us*. That all statements are relative does not mean that all statements are equally true no matter how contradictory. It means that we are related to the meaning of what we say. When I say, "*The Portrait of a Lady* is a good novel", I am saying that "Katherine Lever says that for her *The Portrait of a Lady* is a good novel". The implication thus is clear. It is that I am the kind of person who considers this novel good. I communicate to any listener or reader my quality as a person, not an immutable fact about the novel. Criticism is thus self-revelation, and good criticism includes awareness that what in the last analysis we are asserting is our own natures.

Growth in awareness is thus the beginning and end of criticism. We need to remember consciously that we each have a point of view and that we see the novel as we view the actual world from that point of view. If a novel is obscure, we need always to investigate the possibility that we may be beneath the novel or too far away from it. If I consider a novel good and you consider it bad, the difference may be caused by the difference in the points of view from which we as individuals read the novel. That I think a novel good does not necessarily mean that you will think it good. Nor do I need to say apologetically, "Of course, this is only my opinion". Of course it is. Moreover, the statement of opinion is not a mark of intolerance. When I express my opinion of a novel, in no way do I infringe upon your right to express your opinion.

Finally, *good* is an expansive word. We do not first define it and then apply it. Through criticism we discover its meaning. Each new novel extends or satisfies or falls below our previous definition of good. As we change, our scale of values changes too. We may value a novel differently at different times. As we read more novels, we see that in comparison with a novel we now think good, our earlier evaluations need revision. As a result, we begin to discriminate among good novels, calling some great, others excellent, others very good, and still others fairly good. This comparative discrimination is a complicated process of its own and deserves full elucidation. In this chapter I have been writing only about the way to tell a good novel from a bad. How great a novel is will be the subject matter of the next chapter.

THE VALUES OF CRITICISM

If the end of criticism amounts to no more than saying, "I at this moment consider this novel good", is the end worth the effort of achievement? When we have said that, we have not said much. Why should I trouble to say it? The statement by itself if only the product of whim or prejudice is certainly not worth much. Its value depends upon the process which leads to it. When I write of the values of criticism, I am writing of the whole process of careful reading and thoughtful evaluation described in this chapter.

Such a process has many values, both intrinsic and extrinsic. Our pleasure in reading is enhanced by our awareness of what we are reading. We can thoroughly enjoy an art only if we understand it. Through an understanding of the art of the novel, we can gain in understanding of other forms of literature and also of the arts. At a symposium held at Wellesley College in 1958, students asked experts questions about music, painting, sculpture, and architecture. The questions were the basic ones they ask also about literature: what is an artist? what is art? what is a critic of art? Seeing the relationships of the three for any one of the arts helps us to understand the others. As we develop our taste, we become one of the body of cultured readers upon whom the future of civilization depends. Novelists need discriminating readers if they are to survive as artists. The praise of a few professional reviewers or large sales from a Book Club cannot take the place of appreciation by thousands of good readers. Finally, I grow in self-respect when I can state my opinion of a novel with the modest self-confidence of one who knows not only that a novel is good but also why it is good. Others respect us, too, if we show that we can think for ourselves and do not need to rely on the criticism of others.

If these are the values of criticizing for oneself, you may well ask next, "Why does any one write or read criticism?" Thousands of words about novels are published weekly in newspapers, magazines, and books. Who should read this criticism? The student of the novel. What is a student of the novel? That question is to be answered in the next chapter.

5 · What is a Student of Novels?

Between a reader of novels and a critic of novels no division exists, as we have seen, because a critic is an aware and articulate reader, but between the critic and the student a division does exist. Every critic is, of course, to some extent a student and every student to some extent a critic. The division lies not in the person but in the material read. A student reads *about* novels, while a critic reads novels. Every student has read novels and is thus a critic. Every critic has read about novels and is thus a student. Therefore, we are all students of the novel to some extent as we are all critics of the novel to some degree.

The division between criticism and study has been considered an opposition. Criticism has been dismissed as subjective; study has been scorned as pedantic. Today this controversy seems to have been resolved by the understanding that criticism and study are two different processes, each valuable in itself, and for special reasons, but neither self-sufficient. To read about novels we have never read is superficial. Study can never be the substitute for criticism. That is why this chapter is the last. On the other hand, criticism is incomplete without study. That is why this chapter has been included.

The fact is that the relation of novel and reader is not all there is to be known about a novel. It has an origin in the mind, life, and environment of the novelist and it has effects radiating into time and space. Ignoring this context of a novel is merely ignorant. We should rather see what this context includes and consider what possible value knowledge of this context would have for us.

For the critic reading a novel only one copy need exist. The novel may be written in longhand, typed, or printed. One copy or millions of copies may exist. The critic still reads with awareness and discovers what he thinks the quality of the novel to be. The critical process is essentially the same for the publisher reading a manuscript before deciding about publication or a college student reading *Pride and Prejudice*. But, though the critical process may be essentially the same for every reader, the novel in manuscript moves in a very limited context and the novel enters on publication into a wider context, the width determined by its own powers.

The novel may have the power to attract many and favourable reviews. After the excitement of recent publication has subsided, the novel may still have the power to evoke such strong responses that critics may wish to communicate these responses to others in lectures, articles, and books. It may reach the imaginations and emotions of people who, while not articulate enough to write what they think, still are affected by the novel in many ways. A novel, through all sorts of indirect ways, may affect not only those who read it and those who read about it but even those who have no direct knowledge of it. Particularly in these days of adaptations of novels to other media – the theatre, cinema, radio, and television – people who never read the novel may still be affected by it. They may not see the adaptation of the particular novel, but the novel may be imitated, and the imitations may transmit the original image, even though probably in distorted form. The inevitable passage of time means that novels eventually fall into the hands of the historian either as historical documents which reveal the attitudes of the period or as literary documents which have places in the history of the novel and of literature in general. Meanwhile, the novel may be translated into foreign languages and be read by peoples of many nations.

This context of the novel is the province of the student. When one considers the number of published novels, the reviews, the critical articles and books, and when we remember the history of the novel from the eighteenth century to the present (to say nothing of its forerunners, the romances and tales), then we may well pause before entering this vast field of knowledge to inquire about its possible value for us.

First of all, studying about the novel has the intrinsic value that study about any subject has. It satisfies our intellectual curiosity. The very existence of knowledge to be acquired is a lure to beckon us onward. We need no more justification for studying about the novel than that it is there to be studied.

Secondly, we may justify study if we wish by its contribution to criticism. Knowing the context of a novel provides a cluster of associations which inconspicuously sharpens our awareness. It is in straining to fix exact relationships that we distort. I read *Great Expectations* before I read about the life of Dickens, the history of the novel, and Victorian literature and before I visited England. Now when I re-read *Great Expectations* my knowledge of its context enriches my understanding and intensifies the emotional impact in all sorts of ways. It would be a gross over-simplification to try to reduce to a formula any of these ways. I am sure I myself am not conscious of them all. Every student must discover for himself that his study does have value for his criticism.

The criticism of others does have discernible relations to our own. Sometimes readers, warned that they should criticize for themselves and not depend upon the criticism of others, are wary of reading criticism at all. They think that in some vague way such reading is cheating. Read in the right way and for the right purposes the criticism of others can be one of the best ways to improve one's critical powers. All we need do is remember that each critic is writing about his response to a novel. He is not asserting incontrovertible truths about the novel nor declaring what the responses of others must or should be. Keeping this in mind, we can see at once an advantage in reading about the responses of another. Reading is lonely. Sociable people want to share their experiences. Is this a unique experience? What did others think and feel when they read the novel? It is fun to find out how a novel has affected other people. If the other readers have had a wider experience of life and literature than we have had, we may grow in confidence if our experience was similar to theirs. Others may put into words what we dimly felt but could not articulate. Very good critics can reveal beauty and meaning unseen by us. Even more helpful to me is the fresh approach to the novel that I find in original minds. If the criticism is less perceptive than ours, we can still learn by the stimulation of proving it inadequate or wrong.

A third value of studying about novels is that it helps us to answer the question, "Is this a great novel?" At the end of the last chapter we postponed the problem of how to answer this question. In one group of novels which we call good, we may discern that some seem better than others. Is there any certain way of distinguishing between the great and the good?

One way to begin is with the comparison of two or three novels dealing with similar characters, themes, or situations. Such a comparison reveals as it tests the breadth, width, and depth of the novelist's vision. Virginia Woolf warmly recommends such a comparison:

> Now then we can compare book with book as we compare building with building. But this act of comparison means that our attitude has changed; we are no longer the friends of the writer, but his judges; and just as we cannot be too sympathetic as friends, so as judges we cannot be too severe. Are they not criminals, books that have wasted our time and sympathy; are they not the most insidious enemies of society, corrupters, defilers, the writers of false books, faked books, books that fill the air with decay and disease? Let us then be severe in our judgments; let us compare each book with the greatest of its kind. There they hang in the mind the shapes of the books we have read solidified by the judgments we have passed on them – *Robinson Crusoe, Emma, The Return of the Native.* Compare the novels with these – even the latest and least of novels has a right to be judged with the best.[1]

[1] "How Should One Read a Book?" *The Second Common Reader,* p. 291.

This is excellent advice. Still the question of greatness has been begged. On what grounds are *Robinson Crusoe*, *Emma*, and *The Return of the Native* each deemed the "greatest of its kind"? The grounds are many. The search for "greatness" is as slow and arduous a process as the search for "goodness". We must discuss each element in the context of the novel separately, for the values of each element vary in relation to its nature.

A good review of a new novel can assist us at the outset. A useful exercise for a student of the novel is the reading of ten to fifteen reviews of one new novel. He can quickly observe the differences in quality between those reviewers who see clearly what in the novel has evoked their experience and those who either read superficially or read personal biases into the novel. It is useful to know the reviewers whose judgement on the whole you can trust. No one has time to read all the reviews of every novel; one could read the novel in less time. Yet we certainly do not have time to read all the novels published or even all the novels considered good. Good reviewers can help us to find out what novels are great by helping us to select those novels worth our expenditure of time, energy, and thought in reading at all.

Critiques of novels differ from reviews in being intended for readers who have read the novel. Critiques of single novels are becoming increasingly common in magazines with the expansion of the novel as the object of literary criticism. The novel now has the attention directed in earlier times to poetry and the drama. It is a temptation to think about literature as we do about politics: to think a novel is great if it receives either popular enthusiasm or critical acclaim. The greatness of a novel, however, is not assured by the *number* who read it and think it good, no matter how cultivated the readers. Greatness in literature is not quantitatively determined by voters. Nevertheless, the greatness of a novel is partly revealed to us by its capacity to be read critically by many readers. Some critic wrote that fantasy dissolves out with criticism. A novel is great if it interests readers sufficiently so that they wish to write about it. A novel is great if one critique – even a very good one – does not exhaust its meaning. A novel is great if one critic after another finds a new vein to explore. If a novel can stand up under the close examination of its text and emerge whole, it is great. Lesser novels pull apart at the seams. Effects are seen at close range to be skilfully contrived. The vision is no longer a vision, but tricks with mirrors. In contrast, we can re-read a great novel with increased pleasure after we have read critiques. Critiques test the integrity of a novel and its power to weave a spell which is not broken by analysis.

The context of a novel is determined naturally by the author. Study of a novelist's life has fallen into disrepute because students have mistakenly sought an explanation for the quality of a novel in its relation to the actual milieu from which it sprang. The quality of Faulkner's novels is not to be decided by a visit to Oxford, Mississippi; nor is the quality of Jane Austen's novels by reading her letters. Correspondence with actuality is irrelevant to criticism as we have seen, and it is irrelevant to the greatness of a novel. Even more disreputable to my mind is the use of a novel as a confession on which to base a psychoanalysis of the novelist. This reversal of the normal process of reading is an abuse of privacy which I find sickening.

In the hands of a good critic, however, the study of novels in the total context of an author's life can be one of the most valuable ways of discovering the greatness of one novel. Through such studies as those of Professor Baker of Hemingway or of Professor Guérard of Conrad one gains insight into the range and experience of a man. Each novel is not only an entity but also a part of a whole. Mr Faulkner has said, "But I found out afterward that not only each book had to have a design but the whole output or sum of an artist's work had to have a design".[1] By reading all the works of an author in the order of composition and in the context of his experience, we become aware of the power of imagination which transforms

[1] *Writers at Work*, p. 141.

facts into fiction, of the power of emotion which can be controlled and projected, and of the power of response to changing conditions. One good novel may be an unfulfilled promise: its value is seen in retrospect to be that of a thinly disguised autobiography, and not a true novel. Or a novelist may achieve repeated success with a good formula. One good novel leads to another cut from the same pattern. In contrast, a great novel is one which contributes to the quality of the novelist's total work. The novel is new. It is original. It conveys a new vision of reality compounded from the new experiences the novelist has had since he wrote his last novel. The great novels are not the first novels of an author; the great novels are the ones which have benefited from the experience both literary and personal of the author.

The novelist is first of all writing for his own society. Because a novel is new if it is to be considered a novel at all, and because many people are frightened of the new, a novelist with an original and distinctive vision of reality may be slow to gain recognition or may gain recognition with strong disapproval. We need think only of D. H. Lawrence as an example of the struggle a novelist endures. Novels which mirror society are readily accepted as "realistic". But, as Lord David Cecil has said, "His book must be less a picture of life than a picture of his vision of life, his interpretation of experience." [1] An original interpretation of life presents an image to a generation which that generation needs. We know our own mortality. Our generation will pass away. I as an individual will be known no longer. But, if I read in a book about characters who seem to catch the essence of my time and of my being, my hopes and fears, then I feel I will survive vicariously. Through the novel I gain a permanence and largeness I otherwise lack. I gain through literature a dignity I can never have in person. A good novel may mirror society, and we may be pleased by our reflection; a great novel is a picture of a vision of our society which reveals meaning to us which no mirror can reflect.

A reflection necessarily passes with the society it reflects.

[1] *The Fine Art of Reading*, p. 104.

Only the picture of a vision can survive from one generation to another. A novel which gives us the sense that this was the way people lived in past times is a great one. The survival of a novel from one century to another is a severe test of its quality. Only a few novels can still seem new when they are centuries old. When all the immediate aids which stimulate our interest in fiction have disappeared, manners have changed, the language itself has altered, the novel which can still hold our interest through sheer power of imagination and emotion is to be accounted great.

The historical context of a novel consists not only of the period in the world's history but also of the period in literary history. I believe that each genre of literature has a cycle through which it passes. This cycle need not be considered a development, because sometimes geniuses write during an early phase of the cycle while only mediocre writers are composing during a later phase. The history of both drama and fiction seems to me to be a search for a reality which is neither fact nor fantasy and for a truth which is neither fable nor formula. This is a search each novelist must make for himself, no matter how aware he is of his place in the cycle of his genre. When we know the history of the English and American novel and can place a novel in its context, we can see how original the novel is. A good novel may be simply one among other similar novels of its time. What we thought was originality was its difference from contemporary novels, and not genuine originality. In contrast, a great novel will be seen as rising in prominence among the many novels of its time.

So far I have written only of English and American novels. A further test of the quality of a novel is translation. We have seen that a novel is composed of words. If the very words with all their connotations are taken away and a totally different set substituted, surely the novel itself has gone. Yet that is not our experience in reading the great novels of Russia, France, Germany, and Spain. We can still read with interest, emotion, and insight which lead us to say a novel is good. One sign of a great novel is its power to move readers in different languages.

Another sign is the power of a novelist to create an image of his people for another nation. True as an image of the Russians or not, for many people the Russian character is the one portrayed by Tolstoy in *War and Peace*. For centuries *Don Quixote* has meant the Spanish people and the Spanish country. The great novels create an image of a people and their world. Such an image thus affects the actual world. Life is truly an imitation of art.

At the point where life becomes an imitation of art, art becomes a moral, social, and political concern. The novelist who publishes a novel performs an act for which he becomes morally, socially, and politically responsible. He is contributing to the image each man creates of himself, of his society, and of his nation. He may communicate this image across the barriers of time, space, and language. If he is a poor writer, the image will soon fade and die. If he is a good writer, the image will survive for a short time. If he is a great writer, the image will surmount all barriers and quicken the minds of generations yet unborn with ever-renewed vigour.

Art does not in fact exist for its own sake. Any attempt to insist that it does runs counter to the facts. As readers we too are morally responsible for what we read and what we think of what we read. An adolescent does not need to read Salinger's novels; and, if he does, he does not need to try to create himself in the image of Holden Caulfield. By reading *A Portrait of the Artist as a Young Man, Sons and Lovers, Huckleberry Finn,* and *The Sound and the Fury,* a young person can create the image of the man he wants to be which is his own image, and not a slavish imitation.

The power of a novel is political and social as well as personal. When a novel is published, it becomes in effect a citizen of the State and subject to the laws of the State. The novel may be hailed into court as an offender against morality. It may be prosecuted as libellous and slanderous. It can be banished from the country as an incitement to riot and revolution. It can be condemned as traitorous. We can protest that as individuals we thought the novel good. So we can protest that we found a friend good in all our dealings with him, and yet the courts may decide he is a danger to society and punish him by fines, imprisonment, or deportation. It is unfortunate that officials in every country and every age tend to class the saints with the criminals as "trouble-makers". We are under no obligation to accept one official's definition of a good citizen. Two decisions are involved, and the two should not be confused. Officials in each country have the legal responsibility of deciding if a novel is a good member of their society; readers have the freedom (if they can procure a copy) of deciding for themselves whether they think it is a good novel and also a good influence.

The greatness of a novel is not easily perceived. Many years must be spent reading good novels. A student who forces himself to read a novel called "great" – *Tom Jones*, for example – before he is able to respond to it as good will receive some benefit from such reading, but not much. One should follow one's interest. If a novel called by others great seems to you dull, in my opinion it should be put aside. With steady reading of good novels, the ability to read more profound ones will develop and you can return to them when you are ready to appreciate them. If you force yourself to read them before you are ready, you may never have the experience the novel is capable of generating.

Years of study are required for the reading of good criticism, of the biographies of novelists, of the history of England and the United States in recent centuries, and of the history of the novel. Many more years are necessary to read the best of novels written by members of the British Commonwealth. Then too there are all the novels by Europeans, to be read preferably in their original language and in the context of their culture and history. Beyond lies Oriental fiction.

With study the word "great" expands, just as the word "good" expands with criticism. Every new novel we read either fulfils our sense of greatness, falls beneath it, or expands it. What we mean by "great" when we are adults and when we are children is very different even though we may use the adjective for the same book. As a child I thought *Huckleberry Finn* great in comparison with *Little Men*; as an adult I think it great even when compared with *A Passage to India*, *Middlemarch*, and *Great Expectations*. My opinion is worth more now than it was when I was a child because study has given me evidence to support my present opinion. The danger is that I may forget what it is like to be a child and that I may insist upon children reading the novels I think are great before they are able to enjoy them as good. We announce our values when we say a novel is great; we do not pronounce a verdict. We need always to be humble in respect to our ignorance, knowing that as we learn our values will change. We need always to be charitable, knowing that others less learned than we may be voicing an opinion we might well have had earlier. One statement alone we can make with certainty: a great novel can never be outgrown by an individual, a nation, or the human race.

We can speak our opinion with modest confidence if it has been evoked by knowledge of whom the novel reaches, what the novel is, and what the novel gives. If the novel transcends the boundaries of time, space, and language, it achieves universality. If the novel maintains its integrity under analysis, it has real substance. If it communicates an original image of a real world, it has genuine novelty. In sum, a great novel fulfils completely its definition. To say a novel is great is to say with full understanding that the novel is a novel.

Appendix

A genuine student is not willing to accept any statement without verification. I know that, and I would not want any reader of this book to accept what I say as truth without checking for himself. To see for oneself – that to me is the goal of the student. This appendix might almost be headed, What is the Teacher of Novels? A good teacher in my opinion does not say to a student, "Here is the truth", but rather, "Here are the ways towards truth which I have tried. If you seek the truth, I suggest you try these ways while you look for other ways which I may have failed to see."

Some readers of this book will have the good fortune to study about the novel under excellent teachers who will open their eyes to the vast field of knowledge which surrounds us all. To teach others how to read a novel is a test of a teacher's ability; it is also a test of the quality of the novel. Perhaps the only test of a novel's greatness we need is its capacity to hold our interest at the same time that we read it as part of a school or college assignment and listen to lectures on it in the classroom!

Other readers will have to be their own teachers. Now that both novels and books about the novel are being published in paper-back editions, studying at home is not expensive even for those who do not have access to good libraries. They may already have thought of ways of studying the novel. The following suggestions may be helpful to a student of any age or occupation who wishes to see for himself and to develop his critical powers.

CHAPTER I

1. Read the books recommended below and compare the definitions which the authors either state or imply with my definition.

> DAVID CECIL, "The Forms of English Fiction", *The Fine Art of Reading*, London, 1957
>
> DAVID DAICHES, "The Nature of Fiction", *A Study of Literature for Readers and Critics*, Ithaca, New York, 1948
>
> E. M. FORSTER, *Aspects of the Novel*, London, 1927
>
> GORDON HALL GEROULD, *How to Read Fiction*, Princeton, 1937
>
> HENRY JAMES, "The Art of Fiction", *The Future of the Novel*, ed. Leon Edel, New York, 1956
>
> JOSE ORTEGA Y GASSET, *The Dehumanization of Art and Notes on the Novel*, Princeton, 1948

2. Look for other articles and books about the art of the novel to see if the definitions are in essential agreement with the one given in this chapter. A good starting point would be "A Selected Bibliography of Modern Fiction", compiled by ROBERT WOOSTER STALLMAN, *Critiques and Essays on Modern Fiction*, 1920–51, ed. John W. Aldridge, New York, 1952, pp. 553–61.

3. Read a novel which is undeniably a novel – JANE AUSTEN's *Pride and Prejudice*, for example – and test the definition. Is every aspect of the definition verified by this novel? Is every significant aspect of the novel contained in the definition?

4. Read literary works which seem like novels but which according to my definition are not novels. Because of what characteristics are the works listed below *not* novels? To what type of literature do they belong? Why does the difference in type make a significant difference in the way you read and interpret the work?

The Iliad	*Father and Son* (EDMUND GOSSE)
Troilus and Criseyde	*Brave New World*
Pilgrim's Progress	*Animal Farm*
Gulliver's Travels	*The Three Faces of Eve*

5. Read *The Waves* by VIRGINIA WOOLF, *Moby Dick* by HERMAN MELVILLE, and *Ulysses* by JAMES JOYCE. Judge for yourself whether or not the author has pushed so hard against the defining limits of the novel that he has gone beyond them and written a work which is not in one aspect at least a novel.

6. Read the fiction listed below. Decide for yourself whether each is a short story, a short novel, or a novelette. What criteria did you use? Is the discrimination significant in terms of your understanding and appreciation of the particular work?

JOSEPH CONRAD, *Heart of Darkness*
     The Secret Sharer
     Youth
WILLIAM FAULKNER, *The Bear*
JOHN GALSWORTHY, *The Apple Tree*
ERNEST HEMINGWAY, *The Old Man and the Sea*
HENRY JAMES, *The Turn of the Screw*
     Daisy Miller
     The Lesson of the Master
     The Aspern Papers
     The Europeans
HERMAN MELVILLE, *Billy Budd*
JOHN STEINBECK, *The Moon is Down*
EUDORA WELTY, *The Ponder Heart*
EDITH WHARTON, *Ethan Frome*

7. For another opinion about the relation of the novel to the romance, read *The American Novel and its Tradition* by RICHARD CHASE, Garden City, New York, Doubleday Anchor Book, 1957.

CHAPTER 2

1. Read for yourself what novelists have said about their art. The following list is a suggested starting point:

SHERWOOD ANDERSON, "Man and His Imagination", *The Intent of the Artist*, ed. Augusto Centeno, Princeton, 1941

ELIZABETH BOWEN, "Notes on Writing a Novel", *Collected Impressions*, New York, 1950, pp. 249–63

JOYCE CARY, *Art and Reality*, New York, 1958

JOHN GALSWORTHY, *The Creation of Character in Literature*, Oxford, 1931

HENRY JAMES, *The Art of the Novel*, ed. Richard P. Blackmur, New York, 1934

EDITH WHARTON, *The Art of Fiction*, New York, 1925

THOMAS WOLFE, *The Story of a Novel*, New York, 1949

Writers at Work, The Paris Review Interviews, ed. Malcolm Cowley, New York 1958

2. Watch for current accounts of the creative process either in written form or in lectures. Magazines which may print such articles include *The Atlantic, Daedalus, Harper's, Hudson Review, Kenyon Review, Paris Review, Saturday Review, Sewanee Review* in the U.S.A., and *London Magazine, Twentieth Century, Encounter*, and the *New Statesman* in the United Kingdom.

3. See how the actual world of the novelist as he records his impressions of it in letters, journals, and autobiography compares with his fictitious treatment of similar material. The following are suggested: E. M. FORSTER, *The Hill of Devi*; HENRY JAMES, *The Notebooks*; D. H. LAWRENCE, *Letters*; VIRGINIA WOOLF, *A Writer's Diary*.

4. Compare a so-called "autobiographical" novel with the author's life as presented by a biographer. A good novel for this purpose is JAMES JOYCE'S *A Portrait of the Artist as a Young Man*. Recommended biographies are *My Brother's Keeper* by STANISLAUS JOYCE and *Joyce among the Jesuits* by KEVIN SULLIVAN.

5. Compare early drafts of novels with the final one published or read about such comparisons. The following are suggested:

> JOHN BUTT and KATHLEEN TILLOTSON, *Dickens at Work*, Fair Lawn, New Jersey, 1958
>
> HENRY JAMES, *The Portrait of a Lady* as first published in *The Atlantic Monthly* compared with the revised edition. Also F. O. MATTHIESSEN, "The Painter's Sponge and Varnish Bottle", *Henry James, The Major Phase*, New York, 1944
>
> JAMES JOYCE, *Stephen Hero* compared with *A Portrait of the Artist as a Young Man*
>
> HERBERT DAVIS, "*Women in Love:* A Corrected Type-script", *University of Toronto Quarterly*, XVII (October, 1957), 34–53

6. Write a novel. See VIRGINIA WOOLF, "How Should One Read a Book?" *The Common Reader*, Second Series, New York, 1932, p. 283.

Perhaps the quickest way to understand the elements of what a novelist is doing is not to read, but to write; to make your own experiment with the dangers and difficulties of words. Recall, then, some event that has left a distinct impression on you – how at the corner of the street, perhaps, you passed two people talking. A tree shook; an electric light danced; the tone of the talk was comic, but also tragic; a whole vision, an entire conception, seemed contained in that moment.

But when you attempt to reconstruct it in words, you will find that it breaks into a thousand conflicting impressions. Some must be subdued; others emphasized; in the process you will lose, probably, all grasp upon the emotion itself. Then turn from your blurred and littered pages to the opening pages of some great novelist – Defoe, Jane Austen, Hardy. Now you will be better able to appreciate their mastery. It is not merely that we are in the presence of a different person – Defoe, Jane Austen, or Thomas Hardy – but that we are living in a different world.

CHAPTER 3

1. Read GORDON HALL GEROULD, *How to Read Fiction*, Princeton, 1937.

2. Read – really read – novels. A good starting point is with contemporary novels. After you have read the novel, write as clearly and precisely as you can what your response to the novel is. Also write a reconstruction of it from memory. After some months, try a second reading to see what you have missed. Again write your response and your reconstruction and compare them with your earlier comments. Here is a list of contemporary novels I have enjoyed reading.

KINGSLEY AMIS, *Lucky Jim*
ELIZABETH BOWEN, *The Death of the Heart*
JOYCE CARY, *Herself Surprised*
RUMER GODDEN, *An Episode of Sparrows*
L. P. HARTLEY, *The Go-Between*
A. P. HERBERT, *The Water Gypsies*
VICTORIA LINCOLN, *A Dangerous Innocence*
ROSE MACAULAY, *The Towers of Trebizond*
SOMERSET MAUGHAM, *Of Human Bondage*
C. P. SNOW, *The Masters*
SYLVIA TOWNSEND WARNER, *The Corner that Held Them*
THORNTON WILDER, *Heaven's My Destination*
THOMAS WOLFE, *You Can't Go Home Again*

3. What novels would you add to this list? Would you omit any?

CHAPTER 4

1. The illustrations in this chapter have purposely been drawn from a small number of well-known novels in the hope that you have either read the novels or can easily read them

all in a few months. I suggest you read or re-read the following novels in the order given and criticize them in the way described in Chapter 4.

JANE AUSTEN, *Emma*
GEORGE ELIOT, *Middlemarch*
HENRY JAMES, *The Portrait of a Lady*
CHARLES DICKENS, *Great Expectations*
JOSEPH CONRAD, *Lord Jim*
JAMES JOYCE, *A Portrait of the Artist as a Young Man*
ERNEST HEMINGWAY, *The Sun Also Rises*
E. M. FORSTER, *A Passage to India*
VIRGINIA WOOLF, *To the Lighthouse*
WILLIAM FAULKNER, *The Hamlet*

2. In addition to the above, good novels for critics to read include the novels listed below. I have started the list (which is arranged more or less in chronological order) with Jane Austen, sometimes said to be the first "modern" novelist.

JANE AUSTEN, *Pride and Prejudice*
CHARLOTTE BRONTË, *Jane Eyre*
EMILY BRONTË, *Wuthering Heights*
WILLIAM THACKERAY, *Vanity Fair*
CHARLES DICKENS, *David Copperfield*
Bleak House
NATHANIAL HAWTHORNE, *The House of Seven Gables*
The Scarlet Letter
ANTHONY TROLLOPE, *Barchester Towers*
GEORGE ELIOT, *Adam Bede*
The Mill on the Floss
MARK TWAIN, *Huckleberry Finn*
THOMAS HARDY, *The Return of the Native*
The Mayor of Casterbridge
Tess of the D'Urbervilles
HENRY JAMES, *The American*
JOSEPH CONRAD, *Victory*
Under Western Eyes
JOHN GALSWORTHY, *The Forsyte Saga*

ARNOLD BENNETT, *The Old Wives' Tale*
E. M. FORSTER, *Howards End*
D. H. LAWRENCE, *Sons and Lovers*
The Rainbow
Women in Love
VIRGINIA WOOLF, *Mrs Dalloway*
WILLIAM FAULKNER, *The Sound and the Fury*
Absalom, Absalom!
ERNEST HEMINGWAY, *A Farewell to Arms*

3. What novels would you add to this list? Would you omit any?

4. You can sharpen your critical acumen by finding out what in novels make them seem to you poor. I can hardly recommend novels which I do not consider good, but the following list includes some of the novels which I consider poor.

JAMES AGEE, *A Death in the Family*
STRINGFELLOW BARR, *Strictly Academic*
BRENDON GILL, *The Day the Money Stopped*
WILLIAM HUMPHREY, *Home from the Hill*
STORM JAMESON, *A Cup of Tea for Mr Thorgill*
NANCY WILSON ROSS, *The Return of Lady Brace*
SLOAN WILSON, *A Summer Place*

5. What novels would you add to this list? Would you omit any?

6. Use the following critical questions as guides into the heart of the novel.

A. Does the world of the novel seem real to you?

What is your response to the inhabitants of the imagined world?

Do you have clear and vivid images of the people?
Does each one seem to be a distinctive individual who has lived before he appears in the novel?
Do you feel as if the people were living their lives off

the page so that when they re-appear on the scene they seem to have undergone the experiences they are said to have lived through?

Do you know what the people are thinking and feeling as well as what they are saying and doing?

What are your feelings toward each person? Are your emotions varied, changing, mixed?

What is your response to the actions of the inhabitants?

Do you want the people to attain their goals?

Do your feelings toward the inhabitants change as they act and re-act?

Does the drive of the action hold your interest?

What is the effect upon you of the forging of the chain of cause and effect?

Do you understand why the people act as they do?

In each new situation do the people act as you have been led to expect these people would act?

Do you believe in the existence and strength of the ultimate power that determines the end of the action?

What is your response to the physical world in which they live?

Do you have a clear and vivid image of the world they inhabit?

How many of your senses are involved in the re-creation of the world?

Do you imagine the people living in the natural world, acting upon it and being acted upon by it?

Do you have feelings about the places which affect your feelings about the people?

What is your response to the way you learn about this world?

Do you feel as if you were an inhabitant of the world, participating vicariously in the action through identification with one character?

Do you feel that you are a close observer and an intimate acquaintance of the inhabitants?

Do you feel removed in time and space, watching the world from a distance?

If any character has the rôle of narrator, do you find his narration plausible in the light of his relation to the action?

What as a reader do you know that the people in the imagined world do not know?

How does this knowledge affect your response to the inhabitants, their actions, and their goals?

B. Has the illusion of reality been achieved through a significant and effective design?

What rôle has the novelist assumed?

What is the novel about?

Is any character a hero or a heroine?

Are the characters linked together by a theme or themes as well as by relationships to be expected of human beings?

What is the relationship between the temporal and spatial patterns of the imagined world and the structural divisions of the novel?

What idea links the chain of cause and effect?

How conclusively does the action end at the end of the novel?

Does the natural world have significance as well as existence?

Do objects have significance as well as existence?

Is the way you learn about the world in itself significant?

Is the imagery of the language (similes and metaphors) thematically related to the image of the inhabitants and the natural world?

Are other characteristics of the language significantly related through themes to the characters and plot?

At any point in the novel did you lose the illusion of reality because you were too conscious of the design?

In sum, does the design of the novel confirm the truth of the reality of the imagined world?

C. Is the novelist's vision of life distinctive?

What is the relationship between the attitudes of the novelist and those of the inhabitants of the imagined world?

Is the novelist a member of the segment of society he presents?

Does he talk the same language as his characters and share in their social attitudes?

Does he have the same political and economic opinions as any of his characters?

Does the novelist accept as valid the moral standards of any of his characters?

Is the novelist's belief in the ultimate power that controls human destiny the same as the religious beliefs of the characters?

What is the novelist's perspective toward the human, natural, and supernatural dimensions of the world?

What are the novelist's feelings toward his characters collectively and individually?

What is the novelist's scale of morals? What is the axis of this scale?

Is the novelist aware of the relation between the tiny world he has created and the larger and varied worlds of which it is a part?

Is the novelist aware of the place his world has in time?

What does the novelist believe is beautiful? comic? tragic?

D. What is the value for you of the novelist's vision of life?

How do you feel about the novelist's vision?

(Are you naturally sympathetic? Do you accept its truth reluctantly? Do you believe it valid but actively rebel against it? Do you refuse to believe it valid? Do you consider it too limited to be important? Do you feel some way not mentioned?)

Has the novelist extended your capacity for understanding and feeling?

Has the novelist extended your vision of what is real? good? beautiful? comic? tragic?

Has the novelist enabled you to experience pain, ugliness, evil, fear, and hatred and yet left you with a new awareness of pleasure, beauty, goodness, faith, and love?

7. The terms listed below are commonly used by critics of the novel. I have defined them in relation to my own critical questions. When you read criticism of a novel, you should be careful to see how the critic defines these terms.

Written prose narrative of considerable length involving the reader in an imagined real world which is new because it has been created by the author is a *novel*.

The inhabitants of the imagined real world are the *characters*.

Their emotions, thoughts, sensations, memories, imaginings, etc. comprise their *inner life*.

The succession in time of what happens in their inner life is their *stream of consciousness*.

When they talk silently to themselves, they are engaged in *interior monologue*.

When they talk to each other, their conversation is the *dialogue*.

The physical surroundings of the characters are the *setting*.

The chain of events in a novel is the *plot*.

The relation of the plot and the temporal rhythm of the imagined world to the order of presentation is the *structure*.

The position from which we observe the action is the *point of view*.

The terms used to communicate what a thing is worth indicate a person's *values*.

The values of the characters are their *morals*.

The author's choice of words, imagery, and sentence structure comprises his *style*.

The author's attitude towards his imagined world is his *tone*.

The difference between literal meaning and implication and between intention and effect is *irony*.

A subject which recurs is a *theme*.

The integration of all the elements in a novel is its *form*.

The ways in which the author explores, defines, forms, evaluates, and communicates his vision of an imagined world constitute his *technique*.

The intensity and range of experience controlled by technique are the *art* of the novel.

Your awareness of the art of the novel and the value you derive from the art constitute your *criticism*.

CHAPTER 5

1. Read as many reviews of a new novel as you can find, comparing your criticism of the novel with the criticism of the reviewers.

2. Choose one of the novels mentioned in Chapter 4, and read as many criticisms of it as you can find. Compare the criticism written when the novel was first published with later criticism as an indication of changing tastes and methods of criticism.

3. Choose one novelist and read all his works in chronological order along with a good biography. I suggest ERNEST HEMINGWAY, E. M. FORSTER, GEORGE ELIOT, and CHARLES DICKENS.

4. Choose one social period and read not only the English and American novels of the period but also the drama and poetry. I suggest the 1850's, the 1890's, or the 1920's as interesting decades.

5. Choose a good history of the English or American novel and read it slowly chapter by chapter accompanied by reading

the novels discussed in each chapter. I know of no better way for a student to teach himself than for him to read DOROTHY VAN GHENT'S *The English Novel, Form and Function,* and to answer the provocative questions she asks about each novel she criticizes.

6. List the novels by your compatriots you would wish foreigners to read?

7. Read a good history of the Russian, French, German, Italian, or Spanish novel and read the novels discussed. Or read the European novels being written in the period in which you are interested.

8. Read the special studies of the novel such as those about the political novel, the psychological novel, the hero or heroine in novels, the stream of consciousness.

9. Keep abreast of new developments in criticism and scholarship through annual bibliographies.